Forever a Father, Always a Son

Steve Hall
from

Wes Nordlund

1-26-00

FOREVER
A FATHER
(always a son)

CHARLES WILLIAMS

VICTOR BOOKS ®
A DIVISION OF SCRIPTURE PRESS PUBLICATIONS INC.
USA CANADA ENGLAND

Unless otherwise noted, Scripture quotations are from the *Holy Bible, New International Version,* © 1973, 1978, 1984, International Bible Society. Used by permission of Zondervan Bible Publishers. Other quotations are from the *New American Standard Bible* (NASB), © the Lockman Foundation 1960, 1962, 1963, 1968, 1971, 1972, 1973, 1975, 1977.

Library of Congress Cataloging-in-Publication Data

Williams, D. Charles.
    Forever a father, always a son / D. Charles Williams.
       p.   cm.
    Includes bibliographical references.
    ISBN 0-89693-193-5
    1. Parenting—Religious aspects—Christianity. 2. Fathers and sons.
I. Title.
BV4529.W56 1991   90-49850
248.8'421—dc20   CIP

---

2 3 4 5 6 7 8 9 10 Printing/Year 95 94 93 92 91

CONTENTS

THIS BOOK is dedicated to my father and mother, Robert L. and Betty J. Williams. I realize more each year how lucky I am to have them as parents . . .

To my beautiful, intuitive, intelligent wife, Dru-Ann, who is very responsible for the man I am today . . .

To Christopher and David, the greatest sons a father could have, and to Jonathan, my temporarily adopted son . . .

To my in-laws, Jacquelyn and Walt Lastition who have always been there for us . . .

To Angela Strougal and Dru-Ann who labored through the word processing . . .

To my brothers, Hank and Ken, who have given me a lifetime of good memories. They have become my good friends . . .

To my old friends Jim Miner, Chuck Lucas, Ross McKenzie, Mark Ottenweller, John Schmitt, T.J. Kulcsar, Ron Massengil, Steve Sapp, Clyde Whitworth, Jim DeMint, Lew Fabrick, Steve Carron, Billy Poole, Mike Simmons, Paul Kellet, Keith Crawford, Joe Hoffman, and Don Burke . . .

To Greg Clouse, Managing Director of Victor Books, who believed this idea was important enough to be published in a book, and to my editor, Robert Hosack, for his creative ideas and practical suggestions . . .

And most importantly to God and Jesus Christ . . . the greatest Father and Son of all.

Jonathan got up from the table in fierce anger . . . because he was grieved at his father's shameful treatment of David.
(1 Sam. 20:34)

Dad, there are some things that bother me and have been on my mind, but I just don't know how to approach you with them. How do you feel about our relationship as father and son? . . .

I don't know if you have noticed it or not, but I take most of my problems to Mom. I know that a lot of my discussions are repetitious and you would be the first to tell me. Whether you know it or not—that hurts. I can pretty much expect the same response from you. I guess that's why I'm hesitant to talk to you about those problems. More than anything I want us to be like friends, but you're my father and maybe that's asking too much of you. I don't know why I'm afraid to talk to you about my problems.

—thirty-year-old man

ONE

Fathers and Sons: Friends or Foes?

BEING A DAD is not the easiest job in the world. We need a lot of experience to really do well at it. However, experience is something we usually only get just after we need it. Most men probably want to be good fathers but don't have a clue about how to achieve that end. Sure, we have the example of our own fathers, but they were at even more of a disadvantage than we are. At least we have available to us self-help books, parenting classes, and a greater awareness of the importance of building self-esteem in our children. Yet "knowing" and "doing" are two different things entirely!

Somewhere between the calm, rational logic of a father and the unpredictable, irrational emotionality of a child, communication is lost. We try to connect, but the outcome of our efforts frequently falls short. Most men use a trial and error approach to fathering and they end up with more misses than hits. It is no wonder they avoid thinking about their responsibility. Yet ignoring it does not improve the situation and only leaves our sons in a difficult dilemma: "How do I become a man?" That is not just a man, but a healthy male who can be emotionally intimate with his wife, love and guide his children by example, cultivate deepening friendships (especially with other men), and attain professional success.

Sons have it rough today because there aren't enough males available who are willing to help them become men. The "mystery of our fathers" has added to the confusion. For those of us who grew up in the '50s and '60s, our fathers were often enigmas. They left home to go to work every morning to do "who knows what" and came home often too tired to interact within the family. They disappeared behind their newspapers, got busy in their workshops, or drifted off in their easy chairs in front of the TV.

Recently my two sons asked me, "Hey, Dad, what do you do all day at work that keeps you gone so long?" I tried to explain the exact nature of my job, but noticed the puzzled look on their faces and realized that they had no frame of reference for understanding my explanation. Chris asked, "Well, can I go to work with you one day?" Dave echoed, "Yeah, Dad, let us go to the office with you!"

Sensing how important this was to them, I agreed to take each of them on separate days to spend a few hours at my office. They each packed their lunch, prepared their own briefcases, and left for the office with Dad. I let them each use a vacant office that was available complete with a phone, pencil and paper, and access to our video room so that they could watch TV if bored. After using the phone to call their mom and a few friends, trying out the typewriter, mastering the calculator, consuming several cold drinks, greeting several of my clients, having an early 10 A.M. lunch, and thoroughly testing the patience of my office manager, they both decided that they had a good idea of what Dad did during the day.

While the above example may give our sons a clearer picture of "what we do," of greater importance is helping them know who we are, what we feel, and what it is like to be a man. By not freely sharing with them in these vital areas, they come to see us as unapproachable or worse yet "perfect"—seeming to have no problems.

Many father-son relationships are characterized by emotional distance because neither one has ever learned to open up to the other. If you have ever asked friends about relationships with their fathers, most will say, "My dad? Yeah, he's a great guy. He lives up in Washington and I see him about twice a year. We get together at Christmas and in the summer and it's really good to see him."

Upon closer questioning, it's common to discover sadness in the adult son over the many concerns that have never been discussed between his dad and himself. They may have gained a greater respect for each other over the years, but they have never talked about the hurts and misunderstandings of the past. Because both are uncomfortable with such vulnerability, attempts to broach these topics are often minimized or dismissed, neglecting potential opportunities to experience the emotional intimacy of father and son.

MEN: THE WOUNDED WARRIORS

Men have the capacity for relating on a deeper level, but they often do not develop that potential. By expressing only a restricted range of emotions, they forfeit becoming more well-rounded in their involvement with others. Men have been programmed to "perform," not feel or become. We are what we accomplish or produce and our value is in what we achieve or acquire. In order to survive in this system, men almost have to become distant. In that detachment, we become out of touch with our feelings, our needs, and ultimately with others.

In a recent American Health Gallup Poll, it was reported that "most men feel very lonely."[1] Men do not tend to share their feelings with others and therefore their needs are neither identified nor met. Men say that their families are the most important thing to them, but they do not share or adequately express those feelings. The really meaningful issues in their lives are rarely talked about, not because they do not want to but because they do not know how. Freud once said, "A man must be able to love as well as to work." Paul wrote, "If I have a faith that can move mountains, but have not love, I am nothing" (1 Cor. 13:2).

THE ABSENT-FATHER SYNDROME

Many men are dysfunctional as a result of what I call the absent-father syndrome. This can occur whether a father is absent due to death, divorce, separation, or disinterest. The father does not have to be physically absent to fail in providing for the needs of his children. He may be present but not know how to provide for those emotional require-ments because it was not done for him. He also may not spend time with his son because of marital problems. How-ever, a father's absence primarily occurs because he is involved in and preoccupied with his own activities such as work, hobbies, or personal interests.

Corporate America has certainly contributed to the ab-sent-father syndrome. It has encouraged us to be white-collar and use our heads instead of our hearts and hands— therefore, we have less meaningful involvement with those around us. It has discouraged us from having contact with what is real and has substituted what is artificial, quicker, and often even more expensive. We have narrowed our thinking into specialty areas so that our perspectives have become compartmentalized, causing us to lose touch with the big picture. We have also become inward-focused, pre-ferring to stay inside in climate-controlled comfort, instead of being outdoors and associating regularly with others. Unexpected guests who just dropped in used to be a wel-comed practice with many. Now it is considered an inconvenience to our schedule, if not an infringement of our privacy. Men have allowed themselves to be forced into unreasonably long work hours from the traditional forty hour week to sixty, seventy, and even eighty hours if needed. We have been taught to keep our distance and follow hierarchies. No one gets too close and feelings are kept out of the office. The combination of these characteristics and practices have slowly shaped the emotional tone of our personal lives as well. In a sense, we have sold out to Corporate America.

How does this affect a man's relationship with his family? It contributes to his physical absence in the daytime and to his emotional absence at night. In the previously mentioned poll, most sons and daughters reported that they felt closer to their mothers than to their fathers.[2]

The absence of male guidance in the home takes a subtle but devastating toll on our sons. There are at least four reactions adult sons have when asked to remember the emotional loss they feel toward their fathers. These are often noted when a man is asked, "How did you and your father get along?" "How close were you, really?" One reaction is *denial* or emotional minimizing. I occasionally see this demonstrated in my office when a father is having problems with his son and doesn't recognize the parallels to his own unresolved issues with his father. How true it is that we often overreact to situations that pull strings from our past.

Recently a very successful, middle-aged man came to my office complaining of panic attacks. He was quite self-sufficient and minimized the importance of his own emotional needs. His father had been hardworking, emotionally detached, and unavailable when he was at home. This client defended his father's absence by saying, "That's the way fathers were in our generation." While there was a great deal of truth to this statement, as a son, he missed out on the nurturing that he needed. By not recognizing the shortcomings of his own upbringing, he was unable to give himself permission to get these needs met. Of course, it was not the intent in therapy to blame his father, but to help him as an adult son to change his patterns of relating so that history would not repeat itself.

A second reaction to remembering the emotional loss of one's father is *anger*. Some men are much more aware of their father's influence on their relationship. In fact, they react with anger at the mention of their fathers. They have very definite ideas about the problems and mistakes experienced in their father-son relationships. These feelings are often just below the surface and easily erupt when the adult sons experience stress or upsets in reaction to even vaguely related issues. Sometimes these sons have been emotionally, verbally, or physically abused by their fathers. They carry these scars into other relationships and often wear their feelings on their sleeves. As long as this anger continues, there is very little hope that a relationship between their fathers and themselves can be reconciled. They generally keep their distance, have little to talk about, and limit their visits because the angry feelings return too quickly.

Another reaction of the son may be *disappointment and emptiness*. This is often the result of the pain experienced from a son's perceptions of his father's indifference toward him. These sons regretfully recall that their fathers rarely, if ever, came to watch them play football or soccer. They know their fathers missed their awards banquets and school honors. In fact, they may vividly remember the one or two times their fathers did appear for a special occasion and yet there is often disappointment in their dads' overall lack of enthusiasm toward them. It seems to such sons that their fathers just didn't care enough. These sons rarely express their feelings of disappointment toward their fathers because they believe they will never understand. These sons try everything they can think of to get some affirmation from their fathers. What remains into their adulthood is a deep vein of sadness.

The fourth reaction to remembering the emotional loss of one's father involves personally *taking the blame.* Sons who feel they were a disappointment to their fathers grow up with feelings of inadequacy. They feel like they have let Dad down. These sons often perceive something defective about themselves. "If only I had been smarter, faster, better, or braver." This feeling of not being good enough can continue on into a son's adult life driving him to prove himself over and over again in all he tries to accomplish. It can foster competition, a performance-oriented lifestyle, or a Type A personality. Likewise, it can also foster a defeatist attitude, a tendency to give up easily, and feelings of unavoidable failure.

Denial, anger, sadness, and self-blame are all emotional reactions sons have to the absent-father syndrome. However, these are symptoms of a problem that has not been addressed or reconciled. While many adult sons maintain that their relationships to their sons will be different, there is the ironic reality that we will not be able to view our sons accurately if we are still struggling with unresolved problems involving our own fathers.

Many of us are aware of the Parable of the Prodigal Son in the New Testament, yet there is also a modern-day prodigal father:

> *A certain man had a son. The father divided his living paying his son's bills, sending him to a private school, and trying to convince him that he was doing the best he could. Everything he did was for his son — or so he said. Not many years later, the father gathered together his interests, aspirations, and ambitions, and took a journey into a far country — into a land of stocks, bonds, securities, and other such things which do not interest a boy. There he wasted his precious opportunity of being a companion, model, friend, and guide for his son.*
>
> *He made money, but after spending the very best years of his life he had failed to find any real satisfaction. As he aged, he became lonely and longed for genuine relationships. So he went*

down and joined one of the well-respected clubs in his city. They elected him chairman of the house committee, president of the club, and even sent him to Congress.

Yet no man gave him any real friendship. So when he came to his senses he said, "How many men like me have sons whom they love and understand. They seem perfectly at ease with them and really enjoy their company, yet I do not have this. I know what I'll do. I will go to my son and say to him, 'Son, I have made a lot of mistakes, I have ignored you, and I have done you wrong. I am really no longer worthy to be called your father but could you at least let me be one of your friends?' "

So he flew back home and approached his son, who was quite moved by his words. However, instead of hugging his father and accepting him back with open heart and arms, he drew back from his father and felt ill at ease with him. His father said, "Son, I know it's been hard on you, but I want to finally be close to you."

His son replied, "Dad, there was a time I wanted your companionship, attention, approval, and friendship. But I have my own life now. It's full of a lot of problems, confusion, disappointment, and fear, but it is my life and you are not welcomed into it. I can handle it myself, thanks."

The preceding scenario is being played out in many well-to-do homes and families across our country every day. Will it take our sons shutting us out of their lives for us to get the picture? In the story of the Prodigal Son, the wise, experienced father patiently forgave his son and readily received him back into the family. Sons who experience early rejection and neglect from their prodigal fathers may not have the maturity to so easily forgive. The missed opportunities, sadness, and resentments are often more than a young boy can handle. Young prodigal sons may not realize the implications of their decisions, but older prodigal fathers really ought to. As fathers we hope our sons will not be affected by our absence, but sadly enough they are. While I have been writing this chapter, my two sons have interrupted me twice to go play baseball. Did I go? Of course!

WILL WE EVER SEE EYE TO EYE?

"Boy, am I going to treat my son differently than I was treated!" How many times did you say this to yourself about your dad when you were a child or teenager? When I was growing up, I used to see my father as being too conservative and strict, attending too much to detail, and taking too long in making decisions.

I can recall many instances when I knew exactly what I wanted and was ready to take action immediately. My father's methodical evaluation of the situation only left me impatient and wondering why an obvious decision took so long to make. In particular, I remember an instance when he was trying to teach me how to shift the gears in our four-speed Volkswagen bus. He spent fifteen minutes explaining the range of speed for each gear and the synchronization of the clutch pedal when shifting the gears. I sat there bored, staring through him or over his shoulder waiting for the explanation to end so we could get on with the more important matters at hand. As we got into the bus, my father noted my impatience and let me know his concern about my attitude of disinterest. Of course, knowing more than him, I started the engine and proceeded to grind the gears. When I did get the van into first gear, it jumped down the road like a rabbit who could not decide if it wanted to go forward or stop in place. I wound the revolutions in the engine up so high that it sounded as if it was about to blow up before I changed into the next gear.

My know-it-all attitude was quickly deflated by my know nothing behavior. As I have become older, I have still had to learn the lesson of patience, evaluation, and sound consideration before making a decision. Unfortunately, I have learned the hard way, and it has been a very expensive lesson that could have been avoided had I been more receptive at fifteen. So as it goes, "Lessons unlearned are often repeated."

Now as a father of two boys, I often see myself and my father in my interactions with my sons. They do not like long explanations geared toward helping them avoid mistakes, but prefer to jump into situations unaware of the potential consequences. It is frustrating to know many mistakes can be avoided with a little patience and respect for the experience of their father. Some of the lessons I resisted learning from my father, I had to learn the hard way. Thus, I finally have more appreciation for a father who tried his best to get through to a stubborn son. I also realize he was not quite as conservative and slow to make a decision as I once perceived him to be. Now when I talk with my sons in an instructional way, I occasionally notice the same impatient attitude and glazed look in their eyes.

While my father and I did not see eye to eye on certain issues when I was a teenager, over sixteen years of marriage and two sons have caused me to have a greater empathy for his perspective. I now realize it is not so important that we agree on everything, as it is to learn the lessons that these early situations provide. The older and the younger generations have a hard time understanding each other, but perhaps it is God's intention that with a little tolerance we can learn from one another and grow closer through it all. A line from the recent popular song, "The Living Years," by Mike and the Mechanics describes the difficulties fathers and sons have if they do not voice their differences with each other openly: "Every generation blames the one before."

HONESTY AND VULNERABILITY

There are probably some unresolved hurts, pains from the past, or remorseful regrets that all fathers and sons have about their relationships. To allow those feelings to linger without discussing them or admitting that they exist, keeps that relationship from truly growing closer. Thomas Jefferson once said, "Honesty is the first chapter in the book of wisdom." Honesty is necessary for us to express the feelings we have toward one another. The conflict that it causes will either draw us closer together or push us farther apart. Often our fears of making matters worse contribute to avoiding the issue altogether, allowing it to remain unresolved. However, the price of freedom is vulnerability. It is very common for us to give up after only one or two attempts to talk with someone about a problem we have with them. Matthew 18:15-17 tells us to approach the other party at least three times to settle a conflict and gives us specifics as to how to go about it.

A couple of years ago I decided to talk more regularly and openly about my relationships with my sons and my father. I began taking each of my sons out to breakfast separately and asking them how they were doing and how they felt I was doing as their dad. At first they were surprised and responded, "Fine," "You're perfect," and "You're a good Dad." Later, with some encouragement from me, they were able to tell me other things that they felt. They let me know that they needed more of my time. They told me that they were more motivated by my praise and encouragement than by my direction and correction.

Efforts with my father have also been encouraging. While at first he seemed a little reluctant to resurrect the past, slowly over time he helped me see, from his perspective, the struggles he had with me. He had to tell me things many times because I often disregarded his suggestions. He also had to sit back frustrated over my halfhearted efforts after he had urged me to do my best. I have a better understanding now of his impatience and silence when things were not going well between us. However, I realize how my not discussing these incidents with him led to the distance between us during that time. At some point he must have recognized that I would have to learn some lessons the hard way on my own.

Now that I have two sons of my own and am experiencing some of the same frustrations with them, I have a greater appreciation for my father and how difficult it is to make good judgments when dealing with children. So today as a father I am growing in my understanding. I'm learning that a wise person sets an example of the suggestions he offers, yet allows others to learn from the experience of their own choices.

Perhaps you feel that it is unfair for a son to have to work to change a father-son situation that he did not create. However, waiting for the other person to make the first move only allows the problem to go unresolved at a cost of ill feelings and emotional distance. In my practice I have noticed several catalysts that motivate people to face problems otherwise ignored:

(1) One of the catalysts is the realization that unhappy father-son relationships will continue from generation to generation until someone breaks the cycle. What we resist dealing with persists. If we do not change the present, it will repeat itself in the future.

(2) Sometimes a death, trauma, or significant loss will cause people to come together who have long been emotionally separated. It is as if the more important feelings of love within the relationship surface in spite of the petty differences that have kept them apart.

(3) Likewise, a "significant other" inside or outside the family can sometimes intervene to help two people work through their differences. Having a third party mediate helps feelings and needs to be communicated and minimizes the risk of further conflict.

Helping fathers and sons become friends may be a slow, somewhat painful process. Greater feelings of closeness may even take months or years to establish; however, the reward is worth the risk. Many of us would probably jump at the chance to relive certain parts of our past over again. We would try harder in some areas and perhaps not take other areas so seriously. The writer of the ideas below nicely captures this spirit:

> *If I had my life to live over again, I'd try to make more mistakes next time.*
> *I would relax, I would limber up, I would be sillier than I have been this trip.*
> *I know of very few things I would take seriously.*
> *I would take more trips. I would be crazier.*
> *I would climb more mountains, swim more rivers, and watch more sunsets.*
> *I would do more walking and looking.*
> *I would eat more ice cream and less beans.*
> *I would have more actual troubles, and fewer imaginary ones.*
> *You see, I'm one of those people who lives life prophylactically and sensibly hour after hour, day after day.*
> *Oh, I've had my moments, and if I had to do it over again, I'd have more of them.*
> *In fact, I'd try to have nothing else, just moments, one after another, instead of living so many years ahead each day.*
> *I've been one of those people who never go anywhere without a thermometer, a hot-water bottle, a gargle, a raincoat, aspirin, and a parachute.*
> *If I had to do it over again I would go places, do things, and travel lighter than I have.*
> *If I had my life to live over, I would start barefooted earlier in the spring and stay that way later in the fall.*
> *I would play hooky more.*
> *I wouldn't make such good grades, except by accident.*
> *I would ride on more merry-go-rounds.*
> *I'd pick more daisies. I'd enjoy my sons every day.*
>
> *—Anonymous*

Words to Fathers:
What is your relationship with your son like today? Were (or are) you an absent father? Confess your failures to the

Lord and make a plan to change. Review the "Before It's Too Late" section and resolve today to spend more time with your son. You can not only be a forever father, but a forever friend as well.

Suggestions for Sons:
Are you a victim of the absent-father syndrome? Whether you are a past victim or current sufferer, life with father can be better. Examine the catalysts for change on page 20. Do any of these have application to your situation? Perhaps you will have to make the first step to mend fences with father. Go forward without fear, remember our God is a redeemer God—He can accomplish great things.

Now listen, you who say, "Today or tomorrow we will go to this or that city, spend a year there, carry on business and make money." Why you do not even know what will happen tomorrow. What is your life? You are a mist that appears for a little while and then vanishes.

(James 4:13-14)

My father grew up during the Depression and he often talked about how hard times were back then. I guess that's why he was always working and gone so much. You know, he never came to even one of my school baseball or football games when I was a kid. I'm sure that is why I try to attend everything in which my son participates. I, for one, know how much it hurts to look over into the crowd and not have a dad there cheering for you. It's going to be different for my son.

—forty-year-old man

TWO

Rediscovering Fatherhood

ONE NIGHT several nights ago I had a dream that awakened me early in the morning. It was so upsetting that I was unable to go back to sleep. So I arose at 5 o'clock in the morning and wrote down what I could remember of it, along with my reactions to the dream. The following is an account of that dream:

I had a dream last night that I had died. I don't remember how I died or for how long I had been dead, but I came back briefly to see how things had changed and how everyone had adjusted. Life had continued and people were busy with all their seemingly important day to day activities and responsibilities. What I immediately noticed was how oblivious everyone seemed toward the importance of cherishing the blessings of life with each other. Most people seemed to be totally out of touch with how precious each moment with a loved one was. Oh yes, they saw each other but they weren't truly in tune with how significant that brief time together was.

As I walked around and saw family members, old friends,

and acquaintances, I was struck by how busy they were and how insignificant their exchanges with each other seemed to be, as if they would live forever. As they saw me, there was an initial flicker of recognition that almost as quickly disappeared, and they went on with their conversations as if it were business as usual. As for me, I was hanging onto each moment, word, and experience knowing that it could and probably would be my last time with them.

It seemed they partially realized who I was and our mutual excitement intensified. However, they also had a difficult time believing it was really me. I remember visiting what appeared to be my mother's house and feeling so relieved she fully knew who I was. She welcomed me immediately with hugs and sighs — yet somehow she knew my stay would be brief. My dad wasn't around and I was left with the impression that he too was gone and that my mother was alone and on her own. She had a sadness about her regarding the past and how much loss she had experienced. However, my mom also had a sense of peace about her for she was always a person who made the most of the moments with those she loved, expressing encouraging words of love, praise, and affection.

The next thing I knew I was walking down the street with my youngest brother, Ken. Somehow, he sensed my desperate need to be heard, to feel, and to be alive again. We talked for hours about the family and how I really was missed by them all.

A couple of his friends came hurrying by dressed in business suits and talking about their current financial investments. They each had a look of determination in their eyes to make their "mark" professionally. I recognized them as old playmates of my brother's and commented to them, "Hey, don't take life too seriously." But, they basically ignored me and continued walking. For some reason it seemed very appropriate to say to them, "See you all on the last day." To this they briefly turned their heads, puzzled over this strange comment, and went on their way. Ken knew what I meant and he smiled as we walked ahead.

The last scene of my dream was the most moving for me. Again I was at my mother's house and I was walking around looking at old pieces of furniture I had not seen since I was a small child. All of a sudden my two young sons, Chris and David, bounded in with all the energy, activity, and intensity that seems to be a part of all little boys. They were absorbed in this toy and in that object, almost oblivious to me. When they recognized me, we all hugged, kissed, and squeezed each other. However, as young boys will be, they were quickly distracted by all there was to explore. I was totally engrossed in the moment and I could not take my eyes off of them. I kept talking with them, asking them questions, and trying to keep them involved with me, realizing they did not recognize the significance of our limited time together. At that time I recalled all the people who had told me, "Enjoy them now because they quickly grow up and then they're gone!" Most of those times I had politely smiled and nodded, but I was now actually experiencing that reality. The painful, ironic twist was that I would never see them grow up. The emotional pain was more than I could bear and I hung onto their every movement, word, and glance.

Then my wife appeared with her warm, accepting smile and we both vicariously enjoyed our boys having their fun together. It was so reassuring to see her and feel her close to me again. Immediately the realization washed over me of how much time I had wasted by not cherishing each moment, not telling them how much I loved them more often, and not being attentive enough to them while we were together. At that moment I could not get enough of them. I wanted the moment to last forever. I wanted to remain there looking at it, holding them, and loving them. I realized how much of the past times had been spent correcting, teaching, and doing things—distracted by the goal of achieving some unimportant task and not focused on loving, accepting, and letting them know they were the most important thing in the world to me.

I knew it was time to say good-bye and I dreaded it. I didn't want to leave. It was so painful realizing I wouldn't see my wife and boys again until the "last day." I wouldn't get the chance to say, "I love you," help them through tough and trying times, protect them from the injustices of life, provide for them, or just enjoy their enthusiasm, hugs, and love of life. Sadly, our brief visit was over and my dream ended.

I awoke with a renewed commitment to live as if each day were my last, showing and showering those very significant people with my love, attention, time, encouragement, affection, and especially my presence until that day comes when I have to say good-bye until the "last day."

My experience left me with the realization that all we each have is today. I immediately related to what Moses must have felt after descending from Mount Sinai and how James, John, and Peter wanted to preserve the moment with Jesus when He was transfigured before their eyes. Like Moses' face, the intensity of such moments eventually fade in our minds and we again lose sight of our priorities as other issues compete for our time and attention.

As you read this, is there something you want to say to your spouse, son, daughter, parent, or friend, but haven't taken the time to do? Have you been meaning to plan a special time with your family but have just been too busy to get it on the calendar? Does each member of your family know you love him or her? Do you have any unfinished business with a relationship that has kept you from feeling close to another person? Don't wait! Someday it will be too late. All we have is today, this moment, this opportunity. If you have trouble saying it face-to-face, then call that person on the phone. If that is too threatening, write a letter—but send it immediately before the "last day."

TRENDS TOWARD INVOLVEMENT

"Sons are a heritage from the Lord, children a reward from Him. Like arrows in the hands of a warrior are sons born in one's youth. Blessed is the man whose quiver is full of them" (Psalm 127:3-5). Scripture places a high premium on father-son relationships. Though as we noted in chapter 1, many fathers are failing their biblical mandate. However, there does appear to be a trend toward fathers having more involvement with their children.

During the last couple of years a number of movies have been produced depicting father-son struggles and attempts to resolve their relationships, including *Memories of Me, Nothing in Common, Field of Dreams,* and *Parenthood.* Men seem to want to be home more instead of working sixty or seventy hours each week. Fathers are less willing to remain in jobs where they are traveling five days per week. They are even accepting lesser paying jobs and postponing career promotions to spend more time at home with their children. Some are realizing the necessity of lowering their standard of living in order to spend this valuable time with their families. Even more wives are wanting to become homemakers again.

One article noted that of the 65 percent of mothers who worked outside the home, only 30 percent of these were employed full-time.[1] In my practice I regularly see men who have gone through divorces and the loss of their families because they were too committed to their jobs. These same men are now deciding to keep their professions within limits so that they can maintain their marriage and fatherly responsibilities. With the advancement of the computer and telephone communications industry, many people are able to work out of their homes rather than spending all their time at the office. This, of course, frees up more time for their families. I had one client recently who took his family with him on short business trips out of town. He also utilized a computer regularly and had a modem which allowed him to work from his study at home, interfacing with other offices around the country. He had already lost one family and was committed to make his second attempt with both his wife and child a success.

THE MYTH OF QUALITY TIME

There is a myth which implies that the amount of time spent together is not as significant as the quality of time experienced. Quality time, of course, is necessary and includes a number of important variables such as sharing one on one, talking over problems, limiting interruptions from telephones or others, and delving deeper into one another's feelings and needs. However, quality time is very difficult to plan and children generally resist being emotionally scheduled into a time slot. The reality of the matter is that any moment can be transformed into quality time if a parent is alert, tuned in, and responsive. Quality and quantity are necessary. Children need a lot of time to hang out, run errands, participate in chores, have fun, or just talk. The truth is that quality time often comes during quantity times because relevant issues come up almost unexpectedly. Important personal questions and opportunities to talk often surface when they are least expected. These treasured times help a child feel loved. While quantity time does not necessarily occur during quality time, quality time often occurs during quantity time.

Children, much like adults, need warm-up time so they can acclimate to being around us after we have been gone all day. Questions like, "How was your day?" or "What did you do in school today?" may break the ice but in no way guarantee emotional exchange. There simply is no substitute for time together. This time together must also be accompanied by attention, warmth, humor, and affection. The "one-minute father" will have trouble accomplishing this kind of quality without investing quantity time.

FANTASY FATHER FIGURES

There are a couple types of father figures that appear to carry a lot of appeal, but upon closer examination fall short of fulfilling the needs a son has. We would be wise to avoid these models if we are at all tempted to imitate them.

The *instant father* is one that is born out of the fast-paced society we live in today.[2] Our instant society provides fast food, computer access to all kinds of immediate information, microwave ovens, fast forward on our tape and video recorders, expressways, jet travel, call waiting, one hour martinizing, one minute managers, one minute parenting, a quality time mentality, and credit card access to anything we want. The message in this instant society is that you can have it *all* and you can have it *now*.

This philosophy contradicts the previous generation's idea that anything worth having is worth waiting and working for. The outcome of this instant society mentality is impatience with others who are slower than ourselves, trying to accomplish too much in too little time, greediness over material possessions, selfish ambition in our achievements, low frustration levels, underestimating how long things really take to accomplish, and a tendency to give up too easily.

What is the effect on a father's role in a society which expects things to occur quickly? The effect, of course, is the establishment of an *instant father*. An *instant father* blasts in after a long day and acts as if he and his son are emotionally close even if they really are not. There is an all-glitter-but-no-gold feeling within the son about the relationship as Dad says, "Hey, son, how are you doing?" gives a quick hug and continues, "You're great, gotta go," leaving his child alone once again.

Boys whose fathers regularly enter and leave their lives have an illusion of time together, but feel cheated, frustrated, unfulfilled, yearning for more of Dad's time. Ironically, the sons themselves often feel guilty for the lack of appreciation they show toward their dads and the little bit of quality time they have received. It is very hard for a son to put his finger on his emptiness and anger when it appears that things are better than they really are.

The father who spends time together doing what *he* chooses to do with his child is also creating an *instant father* atmosphere. Most sons take advantage of this opportunity realizing this may be the only Dad time available, yet they may actually prefer to engage in other activities. Fathers need to be aware of such one-sided time; sons should be given the chance to determine father-son activities as well.

I remember coming in from work recently in a rush because of a meeting I had to attend after dinner. As Murphy's Law would have it, my youngest son, David, asked me to repair one of his GI Joe soldiers. My first reaction was to postpone this project and repair the toy later that evening so it would be available for him the next morning. I then realized this might be the only interaction I would have with him for the rest of the day. So we took the ten minutes required to go down to the basement, drill a hole in GI Joe's leg, insert a screw, and render his toy functional. I'm glad I became an available father and not an instant one for my son.

SUPER DAD

A second fantasy father is *super dad*. He is seen as the greatest and often viewed as infallible. He finds himself up on a pedestal in the eyes of his children—almost godlike. They admire him, but have a hard time relating to him because he doesn't seem to make mistakes. There is a price to be paid for this image. While Dad may be the hero, his children may feel he cannot relate to their situations. A father may genuinely intend to motivate his son when he says, "Try harder, practice more and you'll get better." A son may be privately thinking to himself, "It's easy for you to say that, Dad. You're twice as big as I am, three times as old, and besides, it's easier for you." The message is clear: "He's up there; I'm down here. I'm not good enough and I just don't measure up. I could never be like him though I wish I were."

This discouragement often causes sons to give up before they really discover and develop their own talents. *Super dads* often unwittingly foster a fear of failure in their sons because of the difference in their perceived perfect performance and their son's very imperfect, undeveloped abilities.

There are pitfalls in being a *super dad*. There is only one place you can go when on a pedestal. Eventually kids grow up and realize that Dad isn't the greatest. He is fallible and he does make mistakes. Our children begin seeing our shortcomings and we lose credibility if we try to maintain that image. If we refuse to change and allow them to see us as real and human, at least three reactions may occur.

First, they may begin to resent us and feel angry at our emotional inaccessibility. Their frustration with us could cause them to reject the values and lifestyles we have tried to instill in them. They may purposely misbehave and act opposite of the way they were reared.

Secondly, they may allow us to maintain the *super dad* image, appearing as one-dimensional to them with only strengths and no weaknesses. In response, they may try to be *super kids* and please us by their performance. They try to become what they think we want rather than developing the skills, talents, and interests that are their own.

Thirdly, they may pretend to admire us even though they are disillusioned with us as fathers. In my office, I have spoken with a number of adult children who grew up allowing their parents to believe the image of infallibility they had always maintained of themselves. These children have been placed in the unfortunate position of having to build their parent's confidence instead of the parents building the children's self-esteem.

Is it harmful to be a *super dad?* We all want our sons and daughters to admire us. Our children need healthy models and heroes. However, they also need to see that we are human, real, and honest. They need to realize that we make mistakes and want to learn from them. It is important for our sons to hear us admit our mistakes and apologize when we are wrong. When they see us accepting ourselves for both our strengths and weaknesses, they are opened to learning from the trials and errors of life. This helps our sons to overcome the fear of failure, see humility as a strength, view arrogance as a weakness, and be "shame-proofed" by recognizing mistakes as lessons from which to learn.

WHAT KIND OF RELATIONSHIP DO YOU WANT?

Do you really want a close father-son relationship? If most fathers were asked this question, their answer would be a resounding yes. When we closely examine the actual quality and quantity of time fathers spend with their sons, that affirmative answer is questionable. Many fathers, when apart from their sons, have warm feelings for them; yet, when they are together they feel awkward and are often at a loss for words. It takes a while to cultivate mutual warm feelings. It seems that the less involved we are with our sons the less aware we are of their need for us. Likewise, the more involved we are with them the more we want to be. Most fathers and sons need a warm-up period to begin enjoying one another's company.

I have found that it is easier to reach that warm-up point with my youngest son, David, because he is very responsive and engaging. Christopher, my oldest son, takes a little more time. Not only does he tend to be more like me, but he is less inclined to initiate, less reluctant to stop what he is doing to get involved with something else, and less likely to express his feelings and needs to me. While I love both of them equally, my relationship with each is a little different. I believe Christopher needs more time spent with him because of the natural barriers he and I have to overcome to feel closer. I have recognized, however, that I have two very "neat" kids who are extremely interesting people.

Fathers, did you know that if you spent just one hour per week in one-on-one time with your sons, the total amount of time you would have with them over their first eighteen years would only be equal to thirty-nine days? That's not very much time to cultivate a relationship with your son before he's gone and on his own. Yet, statistics tell us that most fathers spend only a few minutes a week in one-on-one time with each of their children.

BE MORE ACTIVE

How can we make the time that we have with our children fun for both of us? As our lives become busier and we assume more responsibilities, our mundane routines erode the excitement in our lives. We may go through the motions of living but we often end up just existing. Often, we just "don't feel like doing anything." Our children no longer see us as fun. If our children are not stimulated and challenged by the excitement of family life together, they'll seek adventure in other available places, like alcohol/drugs, sexual exploration, and destructive curiosity-seeking. We really cannot afford to be boring, tired, and apathetic fathers who wonder why our kids are not interested in us. They're excited about all life has to offer and they are wanting, seeking, yes, even anxiously anticipating ways to experience it. Let's introduce them to it together in healthy ways.

TAKE MORE RISKS

Taking more risks not only makes living exciting, but it keeps us young. It allows us to continue facing our fears and expanding our "comfort zone" so that life remains an adventure everyday. Risks revitalize us. They help focus our priorities and keep us on the cutting edge of life. Trying new things with our sons helps them become more creative and flexible. It helps motivate them to experience life on their own. This ultimately cultivates a sense of hope and keeps life from appearing too overwhelming. It helps them want to push further and try new experiences. Whether they are trying a new game or sport, riding a chilling attraction at the fair, learning to ride a bicycle, or attempting a new social experience, they need our support cheering them onward. People are like mountain climbers. As long as they are looking up toward their goal they can be bold, but as soon as they look down they face fear.

Firsthand experience widens and deepens our understanding of any situation because we have been personally involved in it. It cultivates the courage to believe we can succeed. Fear and inactivity erode courage. When I was younger, I was a slow starter but a strong finisher in sports. I was very fearful, didn't know what to expect, and was afraid to fail or get hurt. After getting some experience, I was more confident and able to let go of my inhibitions and perform instinctively. However, this required that I take a risk and allow myself to be unsure for a while. There is potential for growth in confusion because it makes us receptive to new possibilities. Risk can be a way of life that will enrich our relationships with our sons and keep us young throughout our lives.

Are you rediscovering fatherhood? Make the most of the opportunities you have with your son now. Our sons are interested and even hungry for a chance to be together. All they need is the opportunity and to know we really want to be with them. Try to refrain from operating in the teaching or corrective mode around them and just enjoy their company. I guarantee you will like what you see . . . and who knows, you may have fun too!

Words to Fathers:
If you always wanted a close father-son relationship but didn't know how to begin, it's not too late. Your son needs

you and you need him. Ask yourselves these hard questions:

- Am I spending time with my son?
- Is it quality time?
- Is it quantity time? When did I last sit on the floor with my son?
- How often do I do what he wants to do?
- Do I listen to him?
- Do I share my ideas so he can understand them?
- Do I want to hear his ideas without trying to correct or change them to fit my views?
- What attitudes and qualities necessary for successful personal relationships will my son have gained from me by the time he leaves home?
- In what aspect of fathering am I most comfortable?
- In what areas do I fail most?
- What experiences do I cherish most about the time we have together?
- What memories do I want to plan before my son leaves home?

Suggestions for Sons:

When is the last time you asked your dad to spend some time with you? Do you let him know how important being together is to you? Ask your dad what his "father-son relationship" was like. Did he have any regrets about lost opportunities with his father? Initiate conversations and activities with your dad about daily issues even if it's awkward or uncomfortable to him. He may have never learned to freely open up and share his feelings with another man. God will guide you if you act by faith.

Be imitators of God, therefore, as dearly loved children and live a life of love, just as Christ loved us and gave Himself up as a fragrant offering and sacrifice to God.

(Eph. 5:1-2)

My dad was always quiet and hard to get to know. He was very business minded, worked hard, and expected a lot from my brother and me. Even though I was the "good kid" in the family and never got into trouble like my younger brother did, I never felt like I was "good enough" in Dad's eyes. I guess that's why I push myself so hard now . . . I want Dad to be proud of (accept) me.

—twenty-six-year-old computer salesman

THREE

Like Father,
Like Son?

"HE'S JUST LIKE HIS FATHER!" "His dad was the same way when he was a boy." "He is his daddy's clone." We have all said or heard comments similar to these affectionately noting father and son similarities. It is quite amazing that a "little fellow" who is so young can look, walk, gesture, imitate, and perform much like his dad. While many of these characteristics are genetic, it is likewise incredible how powerful the influence a father's example can be upon his son. Have you ever noticed how children want to be just like their parents when they are young, nothing like their parents when they are teens, and then they become *just* like their parents when they become adults?

Recently, a mother called me about problems she was experiencing with her son. She described him as being quick-tempered, volatile, and rebellious. He would not listen to her and had trouble paying attention at school. After hearing the description of her son's problems, I asked, "What does your husband think?" She responded that he did not feel that his son needed counseling. Next I asked, "What is your husband like?" To this, the young woman replied, "He's quick-tempered, volatile, and would rather do things his own way. He won't listen and no one can tell him anything." I then asked her, "Do you notice any parallels between your son's and your husband's behavior?"

It was very obvious, even over the phone, that her son was already a "mirror image" of his father. Scripture says, "Train a child in the way he should go, and when he is old he will not turn from it" (Prov. 22:6). This, of course, is meant to encourage us to discipline our children in healthy, godly ways that they will imitate as adults. However, we can train them in the way they should *not* go as well; and many times they will follow that example instead. The choice is ours. As the TV oil filter commercial used to advertise, "You can pay me now, or you can pay me later."

Our children will be a composite of both our positive and negative characteristics. As parents we must take note of this and encourage their strengths while shaping their weaknesses in healthier directions. There are a number of examples of father-son relationships in the Bible that demonstrate how instrumental early parental involvement can be.

NOAH AND HIS SONS:
HOW CHARACTER SHAPES DESTINY

Noah was a man of strong character. He was a hardworking farmer who lived in a very violent world. Noah led his family spiritually and remained faithful to God when no one else did. No one had more influence on him than God. He was seen as blameless among the people because of his righteousness. He found favor in God's eyes and a special relationship between them developed. Noah listened closely to God and did exactly what He asked, especially when he was given instructions to build an ark.

Noah had three sons. The oldest was named Japheth, the second was Shem, and the youngest was named Ham.

Noah loved each of his sons and as you might imagine, they had their own distinct personalities. Similar to many oldest children, Japheth was a high achiever. He worked hard, his efforts were blessed, and God extended his territory. He respected his father, Noah, and was like him in his ability to accomplish much. Shem, like many middle children, was quite aware of the needs of others. He was more spiritually attuned and so was specially blessed by God. He and his father were emotionally closer because of their similar spiritual qualities. Ham, like many youngest children, was more reckless, impulsive, and immature. He was not as respectful toward his father, did not seem to take things as seriously, and his descendants were slaves to his brothers.

While Noah walked with God, he also had his faults (Gen. 9). He occasionally had problems with his temper and he could, on occasion, be harsh with others. One incident provides some revealing insight into the characters of Noah and his sons. After Noah, his sons, and their families had spent over a year in the ark, they began rebuilding their lives. Noah planted a vineyard from which he made wine. On one occasion he had too much to drink and fell asleep fully undressed in his tent. Unfortunately, Ham accidentally discovered his father's embarrassing predicament and disrespectfully made an issue of it to his two brothers at his father's expense. Shem and Japheth handled the situation in a discreet, respectful way and placed a blanket over their father to keep him from feeling humiliated. In his anger, Noah blessed Shem and Japheth and cursed Ham for his behavior.

From this incident we see different aspects of Noah's character in each of his sons. Noah was righteous, but when he was tempted and acted irresponsibly, his youngest son's weakness of character was also tempted. Shem, however, was sensitive to the situation and tried to protect his father, while Japheth assisted him in covering his father's nakedness.

Each son's future was influenced by an aspect of Noah's

character they individually imitated. Shem was the most spiritual of the three and was identified as the one who would provide for Japheth and have authority over Ham. The Jews were destined to come from Shem's line of ancestry. Japheth was destined to dwell in the tents of Shem, and he and his descendants were drawn to God and shared in a relationship with Him because of Shem. The Gentiles were to eventually come from Japheth's lineage. Ham's family and descendants, however, became slaves and servants to Japheth, and Ham was later known as the father of Canaan.

Shem's spiritual focus contributed to his becoming a great leader in his family. Japheth's hard work and devotion also served him greatly. Yet on the other hand, Ham's foolishness caused him great consequences which adversely affected his future and that of his children.

ABRAHAM AND ISAAC:
THE EFFECTS OF FAITH AND FEAR

Abraham was a man of great faith. He had also been very successful professionally. At the age of seventy-five, when most of us would be retired and enjoying our golden years, Abraham was called by God to leave his country and people, move to a different land and begin a new nation. Starting over again at this age was a great act of faith in and of itself. Yet, he was also informed that he would be "fathering" this new nation with his wife, Sarah, who had *never* been able to have children, making this an even greater leap of faith. However, when Abraham was 100 years old and Sarah was 90, they did have a son named Isaac.

Isaac was also destined to become a great man of faith. Abraham is often cited as showing a tremendous faith in God by his willingness to sacrifice his only son. However, Isaac did cooperate with his father and trusted his judgment. He may not have been aware of his father's plans prior to their trip to the region of Moriah, but he allowed his father to tie him up and place him on the altar. During this time Isaac was most likely in his late teen years or older and probably would not have been overpowered by his 115–120-year-old father if he had not been willing to abide by his father's request (Gen. 22). Abraham's deep faith in God also existed in Isaac, based on how he trusted and cooperated with his father.

After Isaac married Rebekah, he discovered she too was barren, or unable to have children. He again demonstrated his faith in God by praying that she would become pregnant. Shortly thereafter his prayer was answered with twins, Esau and Jacob. Abraham's and Isaac's lives might have taken a different direction if they had not believed and had faith that God could change things. God intervened at very strategic times with them and they were willing to accept His direction.

The effects of Abraham's fear likewise affected his son Isaac. Early in Abraham's marriage to Sarah, he was instructed by God to travel to Egypt and live there for awhile because of the severe famine which had ravaged the land. Abraham obeyed God's directions but was afraid that the Egyptians would notice Sarah's beauty and want to kill him because he was her husband. Fearing for his own life, he convinced her to lie and say she was his sister instead of his wife. They were, in fact, well received and the Pharaoh himself was very interested in Sarah. Abraham's fear and subsequent lie brought about a great deal of misfortune upon the Pharaoh's household.

While Abraham may or may not have ever discussed this incident with Isaac, an ironic parallel occurred later in Isaac's life (Gen. 26). During Isaac's marriage to Rebekah, there was another famine and the Lord instructed his family and him to go to the Philistines in Gerar to live for awhile. There he met the Abimelech king. Rebekah was also beautiful and Isaac feared that they might want to kill him if they knew she was his wife. They both agreed that she would pose as his sister to insure his safety. Isaac repeated history by giving in to his fears, just as his father had done earlier. Fathers do have a profound influence upon their sons in both their strengths and their weaknesses.

ISAAC AND HIS SONS:
HOW FAVORITISM SEPARATES FAMILIES

Isaac married Rebekah when he was forty and, as previously mentioned, she was initially unable to have children. However, Isaac prayed to God, and because of his faith he was granted his first children at the age of sixty. Rebekah was carrying twin boys and noticed how active they were even prenatally. She asked God what was happening within her and He told her that the boys represented two nations, with ultimately the older serving the younger. After the twins were born, Isaac began showing favoritism toward Esau, perhaps because of their mutual interest in hunting and the outdoors. Rebekah equally favored Jacob and seemed to channel her efforts into assuring that God's prophecy of Jacob being served by Esau would come true.

Apparently, both parents openly demonstrated individual preferences for their respective sons. As parents, we can accurately guess how this made these boys feel. Even today we know that when favoritism is openly demonstrated toward children, normal sibling rivalry is intensified. While favoritism may make a child feel like one parent loves him more, it also makes him aware the other parent does not. Furthermore, the sibling or parent who is left out of this special relationship is often deeply hurt and resentful. This is precisely what happened between Esau and Jacob. Most of their recorded interactions in the Bible involve Jacob cheating Esau out of his birthright and his blessing from their father. Ultimately Esau threatened to kill Jacob after his father died (Gen. 25, 27).

What is particularly tragic about favoritism within families is how each person is denied a closer relationship with at least one other individual in the family. For instance, perhaps Isaac could have helped Jacob recognize that his quiet, calculating, and manipulative ways were harmful and unnecessary. God had intended to bless him anyway. Later in life, Jacob was deceived by Laban which cost him seven years of his life laboring for a wife he did not receive at the end of that time period. We also know that Jacob, as a father, had problems showing favoritism toward his youngest son, Joseph, later in life. The animosity that this fostered from his brothers must have been very painful for Joseph.

Perhaps Isaac could have taught his son, Jacob, that God's plans would be carried out in spite of anyone's efforts to help or hinder them. It is very possible that Rebekah's interference with God's plan actually did more harm than good. If Esau had a closer relationship with Rebekah perhaps he would not have married outside their people's race. It appears that he missed out on the influence of his mother's sharp intuition and good judgment because of the favoritism that existed within the family.

While the evaluation of these family dynamics are only retrospective assumptions, the application to present-day family relationships is worth noting. Favoritism on the part of the parent may help one child, but it will harm others. It is even questionable how much it helps if the favored child grows up believing he or she is better or more special than someone else. It also creates division within what should be a unified family and cheats members from benefiting from each other's strengths.

ELI AND SAMUEL: MEN OF GOD WITH UNGODLY SONS

Eli was a priest at the tabernacle of Shiloh where he had been promised by God that his family would minister before the Lord forever. Apparently, Eli served God effectively for many years in most areas. His sons, however, did not have the same love for God, nor did they follow in Eli's steps. Instead they took advantage of their father's position by cheating and exploiting the people. Eli's sons were also sleeping with the women who served at the entrance of the Tent of Meeting. When Eli heard of his sons' behavior he asked them, "Why do you do such things?" (1 Sam. 2:23). His sons did not listen to him, but continued their ungodly behavior.

At this time, Eli was an old man who was quite obese. While he had obviously done many great things during his service to the Lord, he apparently was not responsible in overseeing his sons' moral and spiritual development. Finally, God Himself came to Eli and asked, "Why do you honor your sons more than Me by fattening yourselves on the choice parts of every offering made by My people Israel?" (1 Sam. 2:29)

It is difficult to fully understand what happened with Eli's sons since he had done such a good job discipling Samuel to serve God. Did he spend so much time with Samuel that his sons were overlooked? Did Eli wait too long to train and shape the characters and attitudes of his sons? His sons were ultimately responsible for their own disregard of God. However, God also held Eli accountable for their behavior. The final outcome of his inattention was the death of his sons.

Eli probably regretted being so uninvolved with his sons by failing to monitor their behavior, deal with their attitudes, correct their mistakes, and persist until they listened to him. God considered his lack of effective supervision over his sons as disobedience to Him. In spite of all the good that Eli had done, his own family ended in tragedy. Shortly after the death of his sons, Eli died when he fell out of his chair and his own excess weight caused him to break his neck.

Samuel also had two sons named Joel and Abijah (1 Sam. 8). Very little is known about the relationship that Samuel had with his sons. Samuel was reared by Eli because of a promise his mother had made to God. His parents were named Elkanah and Hannah. Hannah was unable to have children, but promised if she was allowed to bear a son to dedicate him to the Lord. Eli and Hannah prayed to God to grant her this son and so Samuel was born. When he was still a young child, Samuel was delivered to Eli to rear. Samuel spent his life ministering before the Lord under Eli.

During his childhood, Samuel's parents had very little contact with him except when they journeyed to make their annual religious sacrifices at the temple where he served. Eli actually had the most influence on him as a father. However, as noted, Eli was not at all successful with his sons. It's not clear why Samuel's sons didn't follow after him. In fact, as Samuel grew older his two sons became dishonest and corrupt. They accepted bribes and perverted justice in their positions as judges for Israel. The elders of Israel were very concerned about Samuel's sons and disallowed them from leading the country. Instead, they requested that Samuel appoint a king to rule over them which upset God.

It is difficult to determine how responsible Samuel was for the outcome of his sons' lives. In Eli's case God was actually disappointed with the lack of supervision and direction of his sons. With Samuel, however, no mention is made of God being displeased with him or his parenting efforts. Samuel was a great man of God who served faithfully during his life. However, he was unable to influence his sons to become godly men. Samuel had the same difficulties with Saul whom he loved like a son.

Just how much responsibility does a parent have for the outcome of a child's life? How much responsibility does a child bear for the adult he or she becomes? The questions are difficult. But one lesson is apparent from the families of Eli and Samuel: Living a godly life does not insure that one's children will also do the same. Children need to be discipled, coached, trained, and taught to love God and follow in His ways. If we do the best job we can as fathers while our sons are children, they will have a foundation upon which to act responsibly in developing their relationship to God as adults.

SAUL AND JONATHAN:
LEARNING FROM FATHER'S FAILURES

Saul had three sons and two daughters. Of his five children Scripture tells us most about Jonathan. The only time we hear about the other two sons is when they die together with Saul and Jonathan at the hands of the Philistines in battle.

Saul and Jonathan had an unusual father-son relationship. It was one that often seemed characterized by role reversal. In other words, Jonathan spent a great deal of his time easing his father's ill temper and building up his fragile ego. Jonathan helped Saul win many victories by his demonstrations of faith and courage in battle. He also made amends to others for Saul's irrational behavior.

Saul was an impressive person who was without equal among the Israelites. He stood a head taller than anyone, was personally chosen by God to lead His people, and was promised God's power and loyalty if he would continue to follow and serve Him all his life. Saul was a man of extremes. His inferiority complex turned into an arrogant sense of superiority. He knew that Samuel and God were on his side and yet he had great difficulty sharing the limelight with anyone. He was even jealous instead of grateful when David killed Goliath who had taunted Saul and his army. Saul was also threatened by Jonathan's friendship with David. God had changed Saul's heart and had given him a spirit of power (1 Sam. 10). Unfortunately, Saul still lived his life and led his people by doing things *his* way instead of by faith following God's instructions.

Jonathan was a loyal son and a faithful friend. He had the ability to totally commit himself to a friendship and, in turn, others were very devoted to him. On one occasion he attacked a Philistine outpost of twenty men alone with his armor-bearer. Most people would have thought this was not only a reckless act of suicide, but an obligation to be carried out only under fear of punishment. Jonathan's armor-bearer, however, said, "Do all that you have in mind. Go ahead; I am with you heart and soul" (1 Sam. 14:7). Jonathan's faith, courage, and loyalty won him the support of the Israelite soldiers. On another occasion when Jonathan ignorantly went against one of his father's commands toward his men, Saul's own soldiers stood up for him and refused to allow Jonathan to be executed. Saul would have put his own son to death rather than change his mind and risk looking foolish to his men.

Jonathan saw his father's fear, insecurity, lack of faith, pride, fragile ego, poor judgment, insensitivity toward his men's needs, inflexibility, jealousy toward David, lack of gratitude toward God, and murderous anger, and *still* he remained loyal to him. Even when Saul was trying to kill David, Jonathan was able to maintain his love for his father and for his friend yet do what was right where both of them were concerned. Many times Jonathan was more of a father to Saul than Saul was to him. Saul regularly confided in Jonathan and Saul often took his advice. Saul even agreed to spare David at Jonathan's urging.

Jonathan remained loyal to David, his friend, but did not turn against his father even though he often disagreed with him. He also remained loyal to his father, fought beside him, and died with him in battle against the Philistines. Jonathan apparently empathized with his father's weaknesses and made it a point to learn from them. He could have easily taken on many of his father's shortcomings, but instead he was determined to make those his strengths. Jonathan was humble and not prideful; he had faith in God and not just himself. He looked to the interests of those he loved and not primarily at his own. He did not allow the differences of others to cause him to take sides. Jonathan learned to become a man of character through his father's character flaws.

Our sons' characters are influenced by the person we are for better or worse. If we demonstrate a deep faith, chances are so will they. Ironically, our sons will also fear the very things we do. We owe it to ourselves and them to face those fears so that they will also.

Favoritism separates families and can only damage a father-son relationship. The wise father is one who can applaud the different qualities or talents his sons possess yet still show love equally to all. We have a responsibility to be the spiritual leaders in our families. Our example and involvement in developing our sons' spiritual lives and love for God are the most important blessings we can offer. Every Christian father prays that his son will follow Jesus when he is old enough to make that personal choice. Sadly, this does not always occur, and as we saw even some of the great Bible characters saw their sons reject God.

Finally, our sons usually become a combination of both our strengths and weaknesses. Our hope is that our sons will imitate the good qualities and learn from our mistakes. They, of course, have a much greater chance of doing this if we openly admit our faults, apologize when we make mistakes, and commit to God our intention of changing those shortcomings. A father's prayer should be that his sons will be like him as he is like Christ.

Words to Fathers:
How has your character shaped your son for better or worse? Make a list of his strengths and weaknesses and then examine which are yours as well. As a father, what are your fears? Failure, embarrassment, money problems, witnessing to others, trying new experiences? Whatever fears we do not face squarely, our sons will most likely also struggle with and avoid. Have a "heart-to-heart" talk with

him about your fears and how you handle them. This may help him to face his own. Does your son know you love God? Ask him! Have him tell you how he knows you do. If he says, "I don't know," ask him to pray with you about how to be a better Christian father in your example.

Suggestions for Sons:
What do you admire about your father? Have you told him lately in what ways you respect him? Do you have those qualities? Ask your father how you can further develop those strengths within your own life. Ask your dad how he deepens his own faith in God. What situations/circumstances/hardships have caused him to rely and believe even more in God's influence in his life? Find out what suggestions your father would give about mistakes he has made that he would hope you could avoid repeating.

For what is our hope, our joy, or the crown in which we will glory in the presence of our Lord Jesus when He comes? Is it not you? Indeed, you are our glory and joy.

(1 Thes. 2:19-20)

Dear Dad,

I'm writing this letter because I need your advice and your help. It seems I don't like myself very much and I'm trying to understand why. Maybe I can learn to like myself a bit more or change into someone more likable. I'm trying to understand how I came to be who I am. I know that to a large degree I am a product of you and maybe by understanding you better, I can understand myself. When I look at you I see many qualities that I admire, but some that I don't like at all.
—middle-aged man

FOUR

If You Like Your Son, He'll Like Himself

A MAN with a healthy self-esteem accepts himself for what he is and forgives himself for what he is not. He accepts credit for his strengths and optimistically works on his weaknesses. We all have positive and negative capabilities within us, however, whatever we focus upon we strengthen.

Sometimes fathers have a tendency to "zero in" too readily on problem areas when trying to help their sons. At the same time they inadvertently de-emphasize or give less attention to their sons' talents. Instead, fathers should practice the principle of *catching others doing something right*. It's amazing how positively children respond to such esteem-building practices.

While waiting with my older son for the first game of soccer season to begin, a team photographer stood on the sidelines next to us. All at once the photographer turned toward Chris and said, "I know who you are—you're Christopher Williams. You're one of the best soccer players on the team!" At this, Chris just beamed.

Later on the way home, after his game, he noted, "I'm one of the best players on the team." His effort and motivation during that game had been noticeably improved. Never underestimate the power of a positive compliment.

ACCEPT HIM FOR WHO HE IS TODAY

No one is better at being us than we are. In my last book, *Eight Toughest Problems Parents Face and How to Handle Them,* I emphasized the importance of discovering our own uniqueness. While we all have the same basic emotional, physical, and spiritual needs, we are each different. Each of us has had different experiences, opportunities, influences, and situations in our lives. We are unique in terms of the variety of characteristics that make up our smile, looks, walk, voice, intellect, and sense of humor. We are each a bundle of infinite possibilities just waiting to be developed.

I openly and verbally affirm my children for the ideas they come up with at times. My sons' sense of humor breaks me up. Their precociousness totally surprises me and I often do a double take. Our sons need to see how completely pleased we are with their uniquely evolving personalities each day. Every day is a chance to learn something new about them if we take the time. I recall being impressed by my oldest son who sold tickets around the neighborhood to his Scout jamboree without even asking about what he should say. He must have done well because he won a prize for tickets sold. I was also extremely entertained by the intensity in which my youngest son played his first soccer game. While positioned as a fullback, he was supposed to cover only the area around the goal. In his excitement, he pursued the ball wherever it went on the field. While I was tempted to correct him, I resisted this and instead praised him for his enthusiastic attitude toward the game. This is the sort of acceptance we must provide for our sons.

UNCONDITIONAL LOVE

Unconditional love says, "I love you now," and "I value you just the way you are." It does not have to qualify how we will be someday or what potential we have to be better. Unconditional love tells us we are accepted totally and believed in completely. It goes without saying that we can *all* improve, and those who truly feel loved unconditionally want to become the best that they can be. Conditional love says, "I love you if or when you're good, or you do your best," suggesting acceptance based on one's performance. Conditional love also says, "I love you because you're this way or that way," suggesting that a person is loved because of certain attributes he or she possesses. Finally, conditional love says, "I love you but you're not good enough yet," suggesting we're not fully valued or acceptable.

The Parable of the Prodigal Son is perhaps the Bible's best example of unconditional love (Luke 15:11-31). The younger son did not realize the unconditional love that he was experiencing until he demanded his share of the inheritance and left his family to live on his own. Most will agree that he was irresponsible, impulsive, and ungrateful. His father realized he could not change his son's mind so he allowed him to learn from his own mistakes. Many fathers would have been tempted to reject or disown a son like this.

The wise father realized that there were some experiences his son would have to endure on his own and probably learn the hard way. When the Prodigal Son realized the extent of his foolishness, he decided to return home where he knew he would find acceptance. He honestly did not expect to receive the kind of welcome his father gave him. His father was very forgiving and did not continue to bring up his mistakes as a reminder of his immaturity. In fact, he welcomed him with open arms, gave him a robe, sandals, and a ring. He even threw a party to welcome his missing son home. Abraham Lincoln once demonstrated this kind of unconditional acceptance during the Civil War when he was asked, "How will you treat the Southerners after the war is over?" His reply was, "I will treat them as if they had never been away, of course."

Unconditional love does not mean that we never discuss problems, share our opinion or feelings, or help another learn from his experiences. It does mean, however, that we accept one back for better or worse. Sin always has its consequences, but God never refuses our return to His kingdom if we have a truly repentant heart and attitude.

LIKING YOUR SON MEANS LIKING YOURSELF

You can only give something away that you have, so if you don't have it you can't give it. A father who lacks confidence in himself will often have trouble instilling the same in his son. This is why it is so important for each of us to face our own shortcomings. Most of us men tend to gravitate toward those areas in which we do best because they offer the greatest rewards. Unfortunately, our shortcomings are then left unattended and become the weak links in our characters. When we see these same liabilities in our sons, we are often quick to point them out. When we have not resolved a problem in our own lives, we are intolerant when we see that same fault in our sons.

Recently I saw a teenage boy and his family in my office because he had been misbehaving at home, school, and church. When the father questioned him about his actions, the son became angry and unwilling to talk. We discovered that his behavior had been influenced by his feelings of not measuring up to or fitting in with his peers. During this process, it became apparent that his father had difficulty communicating his feelings and needs. He also became angry when his son would not answer him. Eventually, we discovered that the boy's dad had similar feelings of inadequacy in measuring up to his peers. Ironically, their problems were the same but their reactions were each slightly different. The teen "acted out" toward other people, while the father retreated away from others into his profession. The lesson is simple. We must face our insecurities and work through our problems or they will be revisited in the next generation with our children.

AS YOU GET OLDER DON'T ACT YOUR AGE

Older people tend to be more cynical, distrustful, and set in their ways. If we are mirrors to our children, we certainly do not want them to see the world through negative eyes. However, by the time most of us have reached middle age, we have had our own share of hurt, disappointment, and tragedy. No wonder youth is the hope for tomorrow for they continue to see possibilities in the problems where adults have since given up. Ralph Waldo Emerson once said, "The measure of mental health is the disposition to find good everywhere." If our children see themselves as we see them, it is even more imperative that we see more of the good than otherwise. This calls for each father to take the hardships in life and to work through them to the point of healthy resolution. If we as men resolve the injustices that life deals us, we will grow and continue to see the world as a hopeful place in which to live. This will enable us to like ourselves and to develop our confidence because we are facing life effectively. By liking ourselves we can then like our sons. By facing our fears we can also help our sons face their fears. By overcoming obstacles we become a model for our sons to overcome their own obstacles. This enables us to give to them self-respect, confidence, hopefulness, courage, and faith to live life to the fullest. The posture we should take is captured in the following acrostic:
- **F** ace
- **E** verything
- **A** nd
- **R** ecover

HELPING OUR SONS RECEIVE THEIR BLESSING

Some men go through life never feeling "good enough." They may be incredibly successful and yet feel empty emotionally. They have been affirmed for what they *accomplished,* but not for who they *are.* There are still others who may have done very little with their lives. Both groups have in common the feeling that they have not been given total love and acceptance from their fathers. Their fathers may have even been present for them but somehow the assurance of acceptance did not occur.

Fathers often underestimate the value of regularly encouraging their sons. Our male self-perceptions are greatly influenced by the way we think our fathers viewed us. Receiving their blessing is essential for a son to feel highly esteemed. Low self-esteem is one of the major problems many struggle with at some time in their lives. The feeling of "I'm not good enough" pervades the silent secret thoughts of many men's minds, even after they are very successful. This self-doubt even in the face of overwhelming evidence to the contrary has been termed "the imposter phenomenon." In reality, we are all insecure about certain areas and to varying degrees. This insecurity is part of the human condition of imperfection. However, receiving our father's blessing can help us by recognizing that the most important man in our life has affirmed and accepted us.[1]

In the Old Testament Jewish fathers gave their sons specific blessings which often significantly affected their futures. When Jacob fooled Isaac into giving him Esau's blessing, Jacob's life was profoundly affected (see Gen. 27). Today, sons who fail to receive their father's blessing, or the full extent of it, are also affected in various ways throughout their lives.

Recently in my office I saw a man in his mid-thirties who was struggling with finding his place and purpose in life. He had been through a number of different relationships with women but could commit to none of them. Early in his life he had dropped out of a prestigious university where he had exhibited the talents of an exceptional athlete. However, he had failed to apply himself academically or athletically. He was also a disappointment to his father as he drifted in and out of a relationship with God. We discovered that his life was a series of unfulfilled potential as a result of his feeling like a failure in his father's eyes.

It was true that his father had always urged him to do his best and try his hardest; however, he was rarely there to see his son through those difficult times. In the perceptions of this son, when he did not perform up to certain expectations his father withdrew emotionally. This left my client believing he could only be loved for what he *did* and not for who he *was*. Sons need to know that they have our blessing and acceptance no matter how well they do or they will be lacking in inner motivation and confidence in themselves and in their relationships with others.

Fathers need to help their sons accept the fact that dads are not perfect. We can do that by acknowledging our responsibility for our mistakes ("Son, I'm sorry I didn't let you know how much I loved you when it was important to you.") We can make up for not being there for our sons when it was important ("Son, I know I haven't been there for you at some important times in your life, but I would like to try and change that if you would be willing.") As fathers we also need to reduce the number of suggestions we make and increase our praise ("Son, I'm really proud of you. You are turning into a fantastic young man.") Ironically, it is human nature to solicit input and suggestions from those individuals we feel truly believe in us. If a son feels believed in, he will seek his father's advice.

A man cannot know how difficult it is to be a father until he becomes one. It is hard for a son to identify with a father's dilemma. Only after a son becomes a father does he realize how hard it must have been for his own dad. It is a delicate task for a father to explain that his directives, encouragement, and recommendations are given because he loves and believes in his son. Many times, as fathers, we find ourselves being ignored, resisted, and disregarded by our sons. In response we often feel hurt and become more forceful or critical toward them. It may come as a surprise to our sons that they can actually hurt their father's feelings. This is why it is important for us to explore our sons' feelings about whatever we are discussing by asking, "How do you feel about this?" This helps them know that we are as equally concerned about how we affect them as we are with their doing the right thing.

Sometimes fathers do not recognize themselves how important it is to feel accepted by their own sons. As an adolescent, it never occurred to me how important it was for my dad to feel I valued him. My sons helped me realize this valuable insight when they wrote me the following notes on my birthday and on Father's Day.

> *Dear Dad,*
> *I'm glad it's your birthday. I hope you have a good time being thirty-eight years old. I'm glad you are my dad. I like to play baseball.*
>
> > *Your son,*
> > *Chris*

> *I would follow you anywhere. Happy Father's Day!*
>
> > *Love,*
> > *David*

It is hard to put into words how special these heartfelt notes are to me and just how important they made me feel.

HOW CAN I SHOW MY SON I LOVE HIM?

Say "I love you" regularly. These three words are the hardest to say and yet the most rewarding to hear. It is difficult to believe that people go through their entire lives without hearing these words spoken to them or saying them to someone else. What a tragedy this must be. I often counsel men at my office who have deep regrets about never being told that they were loved by their fathers. These are often the same men who go beyond the call of duty in their jobs, work endless hours to meet deadlines, and pour heart and soul into projects—all for a word of approval or slap on the back from their boss. These men often do not recognize that they are starved for the love and approval of another man. Perhaps this was the love they never received from their own fathers.

I was lucky to have four close men friends whom I initially met while in graduate school at the University of Florida. They were not afraid to affirm with words their love for me. Chuck, Jim, Mark, and Ross are men who will not hesitate to let me know how important I am to them. Our friendships have spanned a period of ten to fifteen years and are still current today.

Telling another man that you love and miss him is virtually unheard of today. In reading this perhaps you wondered if there was anything odd, unusual, or perverted about these relationships. It is a shame that we live in a society that automatically assumes the worst about close male friendships. I believe this is the primary reason that most fathers are afraid to freely and regularly tell their sons, "I love you." I have never doubted that my father loves me. However, it took many years to get him to freely verbalize it.

SHOW AFFECTION

Fathers, do you hug, hold, touch, wrestle with, kiss, tickle, or put your arms around your sons regularly? Affection is one way that we show others how much we care without even using words. I have a big golden retriever who loves to be petted, held, and stroked; he cannot get enough physical contact with the members of our family. Every part of his body welcomes and invites our affection to help him as an animal feel loved.

I try to hug my sons in the morning when they wake up, just before I leave for work, when I first come home, and before they go to bed. The world renowned family therapist, Virginia Satir, used to say that all people needed four hugs a day just for "maintenance."

PRAISE HIM DAILY

Words like "You're great!" "Good job!" "You are really funny," "I'm proud of you," and "You're neat!" are affirmations our sons need to hear from us everyday. They thrive on our appreciation of them. One extremely helpful way to foster this is through *family thank-you sessions*. This is commonly done at dinnertime or when the family is together where each person is asked to say one positive thing about another family member. This places the entire family's focus on one member at a time in an affirming way. These thank-you sessions boost family morale, increase unity, and cultivate gratitude and appreciation for one another.

HAVE FUN TOGETHER

During the busyness of our daily lives, we sometimes become too serious. All work and no play makes us boring and irritable. It is just as important to have fun together as it is to work hard together. Last night while my wife was away, my sons and I were able to place our Christmas tree in a stand in preparation for decorating it. We had a fantastic time gathering the proper tools, cutting off the branches, setting the tree in the stand, and tightening the screws. The smell of the tree and the excitement of the moment added a spirit of lightheartedness to our conversation. We joked with each other, sang songs, and thoroughly enjoyed opening the dusty boxes of Christmas decorations.

These types of activities are invaluable for creating fond memories with the family. My sons and I love to play football in the backyard, go out to breakfast, read out loud, watch movies, wrestle together, and tell childhood stories while driving in the car. Having fun together does not have to be scheduled, time-consuming, costly, or troublesome. Try it. You'll like it!

SHOW ENTHUSIASM

Yesterday it snowed in Atlanta. We had the best time running around trying to catch snowflakes the size of quarters in our mouths as they floated through the air. Our heightened sense of enthusiasm was contagious and before long we ended up in a friendly neighborhood snowball fight. The kid in me emerges during the holidays and especially when it snows.

One of the things that I particularly appreciate about my wife, Dru-Ann, is her ability to feel genuine excitement for the good fortune of others. It is not unusual for her to be more enthusiastic about something that the children have done or that has happened to someone else than even they are. Our old friends, Joe and Vicki, also demonstrate this refreshing ability to be visibly happy for others they know. Being genuinely interested in the events of other people's lives encourages our children to open up to us and share things that are going on with them.

My wife keeps a special journal on each of our sons which includes special experiences that have occurred during their lives. In this journal she includes developmental milestones, cute sayings, or hilarious moments that most of us forget soon after they occur. She has written this journal as a letter to each of our sons trying to reconstruct the event so that Chris and Dave can recall and relive some of their own childhood experiences.

Many fathers in our culture find it difficult to act foolishly in fun, be loud, show joy, demonstrate a sense of humor, or be spontaneous. Our sons really need to see us having fun. Recently my son, Chris, paid me a welcomed compliment when he said to me, "Dad, you're serious just like my teacher at times, but you can also be very funny." I am glad he sees more than just one dimension of me.

HAVE REGULAR WEEKLY TIME TOGETHER

As I mentioned earlier, if we spent only one hour a week of uninterrupted one-on-one time with our sons from birth to eighteen, we would have totaled the equivalent of thirty-nine days together. Thus, I believe that regular weekly one-on-one time together is essential for building a close father-son relationship. If you are like most fathers, thinking about going to breakfast and sitting across the table from your son for an hour may cause you to wonder what in the world you would talk about. Don't worry, there are several specific questions that fathers can ask to generate thought-provoking conversation:

- "How have I been doing as a dad on a scale of 1 to 10?"
- "Have you felt close to me lately?"
- "What's the most fun thing you do with me?"

Tim Hansel in *What Kids Need Most in a Dad*, lists several questions that parents can ask their children to get to know them better. These questions include:

- What makes you really angry?
- Who is your hero or heroes? Why?
- What is your biggest fear?
- What is your favorite book?
- What person outside the family do you most admire?
- How and where would you most like to spend the day?

- What embarrasses you and why?
- What would you like most from me?
- What is your most prized possession?[2]

Hansel also recommends preparing for each of these "time-together" sessions by utilizing an acronym which uses the letters in the word **PLAN:**

P means *prepare* for your times together.

L means *live* each moment as if it will be your last together.

A means *act* as if each time you have as a father and son will be your last.

N means do it *now*. Don't wait until tomorrow or next week because tomorrow may never come.[3]

LISTEN FOR HIS FEELINGS

Direct questions to our sons often elicit that commonly heard response of "I don't know." If this is our first line of approach to our sons, we may get frustrated and give up trying to talk to them. Rather, we should listen for feelings. Recognizing how people feel often gives us more information than answers to questions ever could.

Most of us do not realize that emotions or feelings are conveniently limited to only four major categories of *mad, sad, glad,* or *scared.* Each of these, of course, consists of varying degrees, levels of intensity, and differing ways we describe our emotions. These will be examined in more detail in a later chapter.

Sometimes putting ourselves in our children's shoes and letting them know how we might have felt, given the same situation, helps them realize that we are at least trying to understand what they are feeling. A response such as "That must have made you feel _____ (mad, sad, glad, scared)," can often get our sons talking. Fathers should resist the temptation of disputing a son's feelings with statements like, "You shouldn't feel that way." Time must be taken to acknowledge a son's emotions. Fathers should offer supportive comments like: "I'm sorry that happened to you." "That doesn't feel too well, does it?" "It's hard when things like that happen to us, isn't it?" As men, we are often too eager to jump in and fix the situation by making suggestions. By listening to a son's feelings and giving him support, we affirm him more effectively.

SHARE YOURSELF

One of the greatest gifts we can give our sons is helping them understand what it is like to be an adult. Many times our sons do not realize that we have feelings and needs too. They see us as taking care of things when needed and being able to handle just about any situation. Yet, they often do not know how we accomplish this. We may quote the verse, "I can do all things through Him who strengthens me" (Phil. 4:13, NASB). However, they are interested in how we proceed from A to Z in accomplishing this end.

As a child, I vaguely remember my dad laboring over difficult situations, yet feeling like it was not really my business because it was an adult issue. I appreciated his willingness to take care of the family, but there were many times when I wished I could have understood his decision-making process. Perhaps I did not verbalize my interest to him. I don't believe that children should share the emotional burdens of life prematurely. However, if they have the capacity and the desire to understand how their fathers work through their own personal struggles in life, these lessons could be invaluable.

APOLOGIZE

Parents are not perfect. They make their fair share of mistakes. If we expect our sons to take responsibility for the mistakes they make, it is equally important for us to do the same.

One day as we arrived home and were getting out of our van, I reminded my oldest son, Chris, to get his coat. Apparently, he did not hear me and kept on walking toward the door of the house. Assuming he was ignoring me, I became quite brusque with him and in the process hurt his feelings. My wife overheard us and said, "Chuck, I don't believe he heard you." Recognizing my impatience, I found myself in the rather precarious position of deciding to let this situation pass without further comment or humbling myself by apologizing to my son for my harsh treatment of him. I decided to apologize and ask for forgiveness. With a hug and a smile he said, "Sure, Dad, I forgive you." Out of a very unfortunate situation that could have left both of us emotionally estranged, we actually became closer.

SHOW THEM YOUR LOVE FOR GOD

As a Christian psychologist, husband, and father of two, it is essential for me to start my day off with Bible study and prayer. I have too many people depending on me to do otherwise. I view my time with the Lord as nourishment. It is at these times that I feel most loved and affirmed by God. He enables my attitudes to become focused on serving others. In my prayer time I receive my "marching orders" for the day from God. He reveals to me certain areas that I need to work on personally and take care of with other people. I do not mean that He speaks to me in an audible voice, but certain realizations do occur prompted by our time together.

The first thing in the morning, my sons generally come into my study where they find me reading the Bible or praying. This shows them what is important in my life. One morning, as I was on my knees praying, I realized that one of my sons had come into the room. As I looked up, I saw Chris down on his knees right beside me saying his prayer. This has happened since then with my youngest son, David, also.

Our family attends church on a regular basis not as a replacement for our relationship with God, but to enhance it. I am so very happy that our sons look forward to going. Regular church fellowship is essential to developing quality father-son relationships. Church attendance is a discipline worth promoting.

We also make it a point to try to help others as the need arises. At Christmas, we always adopt another less fortunate family and have the boys earn money to purchase gifts and food to give them. If a young friend is being treated unfairly, they are taught to intervene or comfort as they are able. Recently, we have had several neighbors who have been in accidents or who have lost loved ones to terminal illnesses. Our family has prayed for these individuals as well as found helpful ways to ease their pain and loss. We also try to help the boys show their love for God by asking this question, "How would Jesus handle this?" In any number of situations they find themselves, we try to pose this very relevant question, "What would Jesus do?" It is amazing the insights they have when this question is introduced into a very difficult situation. If you have a young son, try it in his life.

My wife and I have taken our sons with us when we have shared our faith with neighbors and friends. In so doing they are given a firsthand opportunity to hear us talking about our Bible study, our relationship to God, and how we would love to include others. At bedtime we have found it helpful to read relevant stories or parables to our sons that relate to specific events that have occurred during the day. It is amazing how our parenting decisions gain credibility with them when they hear stories that parallel the problems they have had with the biblical solutions we have offered.

ENCOURAGE HIM TO BE HIMSELF

Yesterday I saw a thirteen-year-old boy in my office because of self-esteem problems he was experiencing. He felt he did not fit in with his peers and therefore, did not feel accepted. He was trying so hard to be like them that he was not recognizing some very admirable traits within himself. Identity problems are common for teens this age because they are so unsure of who they are, what they want, and where they are going.

In my counseling, I try to encourage others to begin by taking inventory of all the good qualities they already possess. This approach helps children to realize that they already have the essential characteristics—if they will only recognize and accept them. It is then less devastating to begin developing other qualities or talents we wish to acquire without berating ourselves for what we are not yet.

Tim Hansel in his book, *What Kids Need Most in a Dad*, suggests the following five steps in accepting oneself:

1. Accept yourself right where you are.
2. Know yourself, having a sober estimate of your strengths and weaknesses.
3. Be yourself without trying to act like anyone else.
4. Love yourself since God made you just the way you are and you have value in His eyes.
5. Forget yourself by thinking of others, giving more than you get, becoming involved with others, and letting God be your guide.[4]

HOW CAN YOU SHOW YOUR SON YOU LOVE HIM?

Your love is expressed by what you say and how you say it. Your son will feel affection and warmth as you have fun together. When you show him enthusiasm and listen to his feelings, he knows that he counts and that you care. When you share what you're feeling and what you need, he gets to know you a little better. When you make a mistake with him and apologize then he can forgive you and draw closer. As you show your love for God in all the things you do and say, this can encourage him that he too is loved by our Creator. As he is encouraged to be himself he can feel the freedom to develop all his unique God-given abilities, realizing there is no limit to his potential.

Words to Fathers:
Find something to praise or compliment in your son regularly. You will make his day. "Family thank-you sessions" can be initiated so everyone has a chance to give and receive recognition.

Establish holiday rituals on birthdays, anniversaries, Christmas, July 4th, and Thanksgiving. Looking forward to these annual times together cultivates enthusiasm, creativity, and long lasting bonds. Take your son out to just "buddy around," "goof-off," run errands, or relax together. Asking someone to go with you provides the opportunity to talk and be spontaneous. Review the list of questions under the section entitled "Have Regular Weekly Times Together" for specific things to talk about.

Suggestions for Sons:
Dads like to be asked to "go along" with you when you are doing some activity. It makes them feel you are still interested in spending time with them. Loosen up and do not continue viewing your father as the adult or authority and yourself as the child. Try to relate to him as a friend and peer since you are both adults. Be humorous, show enthusiasm. Be yourself.

Fathers also want very much to be reminded of how cared for, admired, and appreciated they are. Your compliments mean a lot especially if your dad is retired and he is not getting the recognition his job used to afford him. Share with him your fears and struggles. Find out how he used to handle those feelings related to difficult situations you are encountering.

Finally, show affection with hugs, an arm around the shoulder, and pats on the back. The older generation may be uncomfortable with being touched but they need it. Do not let their discomfort with closeness stop you from giving them that affirmation.

It is right for me to feel this way about all of you, since I have you in my heart.

(Phil. 1:7)

Dear Dr. Williams,

I wanted to write you a follow-up letter to let you know how my talk with Dad went. As you know, I went home for his seventy-fourth birthday and we eventually found an opportunity to talk alone. I asked him what it was like being a father in the '50s and why he wasn't around very much when I was a boy. He explained how he had to work all the time to just support the eight of us. I told him I wished we could have been closer then. He reflected on how hard it was to get to know me as a boy because I seemed so distant and he didn't know how to reach me. I never realized I could have been part of the problem. I am beginning to accept that feelings toward others must be expressed and talked through. Relationships are a two-way street even between a father and a young son. I still have a lot to learn in this area of life. Thanks again for all your help.

—thirty-five-year-old corporate executive

FIVE

Expressing Feelings: Strength or Weakness?

THE MOST COMMON complaint or disappointment I hear about men from their wives and children is how poorly they express their feelings. Wives genuinely want to know how various situations affect their husbands. And sons look to their fathers for clues about how they, as males, should react emotionally.

Are emotions really that important to express? Many men have seen the effect of out-of-control emotions and the damage they can cause. Consequently, they may tend to limit their expression of certain feelings. For instance, if a man grew up with a mother or father who regularly screamed, cried, or expressed fear, he probably will avoid situations that might elicit these reactions within himself. He may feel all of these emotions, but he will keep them under such control that eventually he may even deny that these emotions exist.

Women who grew up in dysfunctional homes may also suffer in expressing their feelings. It is not uncommon for a young girl to act out the role of an adult in an effort to make things better for her parents. The term for this is "codependency," and it represents the abnormal effort of one person to try and solve problems that are more legitimately someone else's. This process of being too helpful as a child fosters a pattern in a woman of doing more for others, especially a husband, than she expects him to do for himself. Consequently, these women feel and express most of the emotions in the family and allow or settle for their husbands' emotional inactivity and unavailability.

When wives finally do become impatient with this inequitable arrangement, they often express their dissatisfaction in irrational outbursts of emotion. The excessive display of emotion only further reinforces wives' beliefs that it is destructive, unnecessary, unproductive, and even weak to give way to any significant expression of feelings.

But why do men think that the expression of certain emotions is a sign of weakness? Probably because most men have been taught that they should know how to handle almost any situation without fear. Intellectually, they know this is not only unhealthy but impossible; however, emotionally there is something within most men that causes them mild feelings of panic when they face uncertainty. Therefore, men invest an inordinate amount of time learning how to solve problems to remain in control. Men clearly do not respect other men who become too angry, paralyzed by fear, or overwhelmed with sadness. They distance themselves from these feelings and learn other ways to adapt. Unfortunately, this promotes the insidious effect of denial in their lives. By inhibiting the natural expression of their feelings, they become emotionally anesthetized and out of touch with others. They may be able to express humor or various forms of anger, but emotions such as sadness and fear are more difficult to identify or acknowledge. Ultimately, this has an eroding effect on their sensitivity to their own needs as well as those of others.

The more men are out of touch with their feelings, the

less able they are to relate to others. Men are also less likely to seek help for this problem. Why is this? One psychologist feels that there are four major factors that contribute to men's reluctance to seek help: (1) difficulty in admitting the existence of a problem, (2) difficulty in actually asking for help, (3) difficulty in identifying and processing emotional states, and (4) the fear of intimacy.[1]

Jesus reminded us, "Come to Me all you who are weary and burdened and I will give you rest. Take My yoke upon you and learn from Me for I am gentle and humble in heart, and you will find rest for your souls. For My yoke is easy and My burden is light" (Matt. 11:28-30). He knew long before the findings of modern medicine how unhealthy it was for us not to recognize the seriousness of our problems. Jesus also knew that we needed help in spite of the fact that we try to solve so many of our own situations. Men are often afraid to admit that they cannot handle certain things, although this has been the case since the beginning of time. But Jesus promises to treat us gently without making us feel humiliated because of our weaknesses. With His help problems may still be burdens; however, they are manageable.

HOW WE SIDESTEP OUR FEELINGS

As a psychologist I know how important our feelings are in helping us understand ourselves. Yet, as a man I still struggle with discomfort in openly expressing my deepest emotions and needs. Men _avoid_ their feelings in numerous ways. We _rationalize_ not talking about our feelings by saying to ourselves, "What good is it to talk about this? It's not going to change anything." Sometimes we _ignore_ what we feel and wonder why we worry so much. We _minimize_ the importance of these feelings, expecting them to pass with time. Many men stay so _busy_ that they do not realize what they are feeling. We also _change one feeling into another._ For example, by acting angry when we are really hurt.

At other times we merely _deny_ our feelings. These are but some of the tactics in the male arsenal.

Last week in my office I saw a couple who were having marital problems. The wife was constantly critical of her husband because he spent more time hunting than he did at home. When I asked him how he felt about her persistent complaints, he said it didn't bother him. He denied that it made him angry. Upon further examination he was finally able to admit that it did bother him at times. Eventually, he was able to see that being "bothered" did signify some anger on his part toward his wife. The identification of this emotion enabled them to see their needs more clearly and develop a greater potential for closeness within the relationship.

There are still other tricks males use to sidestep their emotions. As men we also _dull_ our feelings with silence, laughter, indifference, or alcohol. The most common reaction to feelings in men is to _intellectualize_ them. We replace our feelings with thought and logic discussing potentially intense issues in a rational, somewhat evaluative manner. We _vicariously_ experience feelings. It is very common to see a quiet, easy-going husband and a vivacious, talkative wife. Do you really think this is merely a mismatch? I believe many men want to experience their feelings more openly and so are drawn to a spouse who more easily expresses her feelings. Therefore, they vicariously enjoy life through the safety of the emotions their wives express.[2]

SYMPTOMS OF DIMINISHED EMOTIONAL INTIMACY

Men who do not openly and freely express their feelings eventually lose the capacity for doing so. Feelings are the major mechanism through which we emotionally connect and identify with others. In short, our inability to express emotions seriously hampers our capacity to be emotionally intimate with others.

Below is a list of twenty-five symptoms that are considered barriers to emotional closeness. In my practice, I generally have men read through these symptoms and check the items with which they have problems. I also have their spouses go through and do the same. My experience is that if ten or more of these symptoms are indicated, there is a high probability that this man has a significantly diminished capacity for emotional intimacy:

1. Generally demonstrates a restricted range of expressed emotions.
2. A limited ability to empathize with the feelings and needs of others and so reactions tend to be:
   a. rational, cognitive, and detached.
   b. an imparting of "black or white" (concrete) solutions in an attempt to "fix" the problem.
   c. devoid of understanding and emotional support.
   d. disqualifying of another's feelings (e.g., "You shouldn't feel that way.").
3. Unaware of own emotional needs so he has difficulty receiving support, input, or help from others.
4. Has inner feeling of "not being good enough."
5. One's value or self-worth are tied to a performance-orientation of high achievement, accomplishments, and acquisitions.
6. Compulsively busy at work, projects, play, etc. which keeps him from being vulnerable or having deep emotional involvements in relationships.
7. Tends to avoid conflicts and "people-please" rather than express legitimate feelings about a problem.
8. Has acquaintances but generally no "local" best friends with whom he has regular contact.
9. Competition with other men (professionally and financially) to gain their respect and admiration replaces the more legitimate emotional need for true friendships.

10. Has difficulty having fun or being spontaneous.
11. High reliance on female partner to set the tone for emotional involvement and inten-sity.
12. Feels hurt inwardly in conflictual interactions with others, but outwardly only demonstrates anger or blame toward others.
13. Has a high probability of compulsive addictive behaviors or habits (alcohol, work, activities, eating, drugs, caffeine, or smoking).
14. Excessive level of self-focus: self-centered, self-motivated, self-destructive, self-sufficient, self-serving, ambitious, or self-protecting.
15. A need to be "in control" by orchestrating his environment and others or by emotional detachment.
16. Feels a combined fear of authority and failure.
17. Possesses masked depressive features which surface when status drops, performance fails, or relationships end.
18. Impatience and intolerance toward problem characteristics in one's child that are similar to his own past or present personal problems.
19. A tendency to "sexualize" attention, affection, and emotional closeness from one's spouse.
20. Difficulty in just spending time together without a purpose.
21. Reluctance to openly disclose insecurities to others for fear that they may be interpreted as weaknesses.
22. Tends to minimize the seriousness of problems within a relationship ("Our problems aren't really that bad").
23. Wife is often the only best friend he has.
24. Tends to insist on doing things "his way."
25. Usually has a delayed emotional reaction over being hurt or disappointed that he often plays down or minimizes. This often obscures the cause of his feelings and therefore, hampers the timely and appropriate resolution of problems.

THE FOUR TYPES OF EMOTIONS

I used to wonder if it were really possible to understand emotions. There seemed to be so many types of feelings it was hard to make sense of them all. Because emotions are so contagious, the way one person feels affects the reactions of another. We sometimes even mislabel each other's feelings based on how we might respond. At other times we may try to find out the cause of someone's feelings without realizing we misinterpreted which emotion they actually were experiencing.

Feelings seem complex and confusing yet, they can be very simple. As we noted, most emotions can be categorized into four types: _mad, sad, glad,_ and _scared._ You may be skeptical about how inclusive these four really are; however, they actually do provide the major categories under which most feeling states fall.

I'M MAD

Anger is probably the most commonly expressed emotion. This is because it is the safe emotion. It is safe because it usually represents a surface emotion which hides deeper, more vulnerable feelings. There is rarely a time when a person feels anger only. Generally anger masks the deeper emotions of hurt or fear. When my middle brother, Hank, was a teenager he was known for his quick temper. Not until years later did I realize that much of his anger was hiding his feelings of hurt. Hank was a more sensitive person when we were younger and so things affected him deeply.

Often when people react with anger it frightens us, and we mistakenly react similarly matching anger for anger. By doing this we miss the deeper cause of their behavior and the opportunity for understanding what they really need. I frequently talk to men who do not realize that they are angry. When directly questioned about feeling angry, they generally deny it. However, if I ask them if they are irritated, upset, frustrated, aggravated, impatient, or "ticked off," they often acknowledge this. When they realize that any of these feelings are a form of anger, they more readily accept that they are in fact mad. We can then identify the cause of their anger and ultimately decide what they need to do to resolve this. While some men do not even recognize that they are angry, others know they are and use it to manipulate situations. Wives and family members who are intimidated by an angry husband or father and so avoid directly discussing problems, inadvertently teach these men that anger is a viable means through which to control others.

Jesus was able to express His emotions clearly, helpfully, and directly. The Pharisees were closely watching Jesus to see if He would heal a crippled man thereby breaking the law which forbade any type of work on the Sabbath. Jesus asked, "Which is lawful on the Sabbath: to do good or do evil, to save life or kill?" (Mark 3:4) He then looked at them in anger because they were stubborn and lacked empathy for the man Jesus was about to heal. His anger was quite justified because they placed their petty laws above a sick, less fortunate person.

What is the main purpose of anger? It appears to be a catalyst that when experienced, motivates a person to solve the problem that has elicited the anger. When it is used for this purpose, it is helpful and healthy. However, if it is repressed and internalized it can be harmful. Likewise, if it is freely and destructively vented, it can harm other people. This is ultimately the outcome of repressing anger and denying its existence within us.

When asking children I am working with how they feel, I often get the response, "I don't know," or sometimes even silence. I then begin using yes or no questions that relate to how they feel such as, "Do you feel glad?" If something is bothering them, most children will say no. Then I will ask about the safe emotion, "Do you feel mad?" If they can acknowledge this much, it is just a matter of trial and error until we discover what it is that has upset them. If I still receive uncooperative responses, I may self-disclose and tell them, "If that happened to me I would feel mad! In fact, one time when I was your age . . . " This actually gives them permission to express having a feeling that you also have experienced. If I receive an affirmation about their anger, I may proceed further and ask, "Did you feel sad or did you feel scared?"

Then I explore the specifics of these responses. Children, like adults, will often tell you that they feel mad before they are willing to discuss feelings of sadness or fear.

I FEEL SAD

Sadness also comes in a variety of forms such as feeling low, depressed, discouraged, blue, alone, empty, hurt, disappointed, numb, ashamed, or humiliated. Each of these forms expresses a different shade of sadness. The identification of sadness within an individual is particularly important because its denial often causes a numbing effect that can foster a delayed reaction to experiencing emotions.

People who have minimized the seriousness of hurt feelings in their lives often become anesthetized to their emotions. You may hear them say, "Oh, that didn't hurt," "It doesn't bother me," "That doesn't matter," or "Don't worry about it." Some of the deepest depression that adults feel is as a result of many years of denying sad feelings that they have experienced from painful situations in their lives.

When men do not identify these hurts or disappointments, they become very susceptible to "self-pity." Adult children of alcoholics, in particular, often have this de-

layed emotional reaction because of years of disappointments experienced within their families. Constantly minimizing the significance of how different events affect us
contributes to the eventual loss of our sensitivity to our
own needs and feelings.

Jesus allowed himself to feel sadness and was very aware
of what caused it (see John 11:32-36). When His friend
Lazarus died, He came and saw Mary, his sister, and his
friends crying. Jesus was saddened by their own loss as well
as His own and He openly wept. The capacity to express
sadness helps us to empathize with and support others. It
also allows us to accept our losses and come to terms with
our own pain.

I AM SO GLAD

Gladness also comes in various forms of feeling happy,
encouraged, elated, excited, enthusiastic, joyful, pleased,
or humored. Gladness is easily eroded if we do not freely
express the other three basic emotions. A man who has
lost his sense of humor, twinkle in the eye, or quick wit is
probably not utilizing his other emotions in a healthy manner. We have already noted that feelings are catalysts for
identifying and solving problems and getting our needs
met. If these needs are not met, it is very difficult to feel
optimistic about life. We know that humor heals, so the
lack of it robs us of its rejuvenating effects. Jesus was
amazed at the faith of the centurion who knew with a word
his servant would be healed. The centurion's depth of belief greatly encouraged and refreshed Jesus (Matt. 8:5-13).

I'M SCARED!

Late one night my wife and I were coming out of a major
hotel in downtown Atlanta after attending a church ban-

quet. As we were making our way out of the hotel, I noticed three young men following close behind us. Rather than walk out of the building to our car, I decided to stop in the lobby to observe what they were going to do. As I expected, they stopped a short distance from us. I decided to leave my wife inside next to a security officer and walk outdoors to see if any of them pursued. No one followed so I quickly got the car and brought it around to the front entrance. About the same time they all exited the building and walked directly in front of my car. One of them glared at me, as I watched him walk past, as if he were thinking, "Wait till next time."

While on one hand, I was extremely angered by the possibility of being attacked or robbed, I was also terrified at how vulnerable we would have been had I not noticed their suspicious behavior. In this instance my cautiousness about the downtown area and the precautions I took are examples of healthy fear. Fear can be a helpful emotion when we are attentive and responsive to it. Fear is the beginning of knowledge (see Ps. 111:10).

Fear can become unhealthy and even dangerous if we ignore, avoid, or become paralyzed by it. In a recent television movie, "My Brother's Wife," John Ritter, the oldest son of a successful businessman, felt his father did not accept him. Instead of facing his father and working through their issues, he spent his entire life rebelling against his father's lifestyle and embarrassing him. They subsequently had no contact for many years. Finally, after the oldest son had become successful, he came back to try and make amends with his father. However, too much time, hurt, and resentment had occurred between them and the reconciliation attempt failed much to the son's disappointment. The father was afraid to change and accept his son for who he was instead of what he wanted him to become. His son was afraid to let his dad know that his anger was a disguise for his deep hurt and need to be close to his father. The fears in both of these men contributed to a lifetime of emotional separation which was never resolved.

The '80s seemed best characterized as the "age of anxiety." In this past decade anxiety-related disorders rivaled the number one emotional problem, depression, for the first time. The me generation's self-centered philosophy of the '70s actually set the stage for these anxiety problems. It fostered a greater sense of isolation and loneliness which has in turn contributed to widespread insecurity and fearfulness in people. There are more people today who are single, divorced, or living alone than ever before. Men are generally afraid of close friendships with other men and often have no "best friend." Fear is the enemy of faith, hope, and love, the three elements which cultivate and maintain relationships.

WHY IS EXPRESSING FEELINGS IMPORTANT?

Feelings are catalysts. They motivate us. They help us recognize what has affected us and how. The feelings that are generated from life situations help us to respond to our needs appropriately. Feelings help solve problems and create a healthy environment for us. If we deny or ignore our feelings for too long, we become oppressed by the weight of unresolved conflicts. By expressing our feelings we clear the air and resolve problems.

Feelings also bring us closer to other people. When we relate our feelings to others we bond together and foster intimacy. Feelings also build our confidence in ourselves. By trusting our feelings, we can intuitively know that our assessment of a situation is accurate. This causes us to believe more in ourselves and develop our judgment. This generates strong feelings of security.

Feelings also help us to make the right decisions. By listening equally to our heart and our head, we are able to assess emotions that a situation elicits and rationally evaluate the facts related to the pending decision.

Feelings also help us to forgive and heal. All of us have

been hurt emotionally sometime during our lives. Recognizing these feelings can motivate us to remedy these unresolved issues. This helps us complete the unfinished business we have with other people and heal emotionally from these situations.

Finally, feelings teach us about ourselves. They help us realize how we react to certain situations so that we can find better ways to handle them. If we become angry quickly, hurt easily, or affected seriously by stress we can make adjustments to our lifestyle so that unpredictable dilemmas do not totally overwhelm us.[3]

WHY ARE MEN UNCOMFORTABLE
WITH THEIR FEELINGS?

We are so afraid of being hurt that we often give up trying to be close to each other. It is too risky and takes effort we could channel toward other things we feel more emotionally safe with such as work or hobbies. As our trust in others decreases, an interesting paradox occurs. The more we become self-absorbed or self-sufficient, the less in touch with our feelings and needs we become. Therefore, the less capable we are of experiencing emotional intimacy with others. The price of the freedom to experience all our emotions is vulnerability or a willingness to risk. This requires a courage that only God can truly give.

HOW TO GET IN TOUCH WITH YOUR FEELINGS

When men recognize and acknowledge that they do not comfortably or freely express their entire range of emotions, they generally want to know how to accomplish this. In my practice I use a specific exercise to help men get used to identifying and expressing their feelings every day. This activity is called the "Emotional Diary." A sample is included on page 86.

EMOTIONAL DIARY

Briefly answer these three questions at the end of each day using as many of the groups of emotions as are relevant.

1. How did I feel this morning?
2. What significant events or incidents occurred today, and how did I feel about them?
3. How do I feel this evening?

GROUPS OF EMOTIONS:
MAD/SAD/GLAD/SCARED
(You may use more than one section if needed)

Date: _____

Date: _____

Date: _____

Date: _____

The above format attempts to get the participant to ask himself three questions that have to do with recalling his feeling states at three times during the day. He is to use the four categories of emotions (mad, sad, glad, scared) in his own words. For instance, if you woke up and felt impatient, short, or irritable, your emotional state would most likely have been mad. If you came home worn out, listless, quiet, unmotivated, or apathetic, your emotional state might be sad. Nevertheless, you are to answer these three questions in writing at the end of each day for several weeks. By the end of the first or second week, a pattern of emotions should begin to emerge. You should review the sheet with your spouse or someone who can help you see what emotions you typically utilize, which ones you avoid, and perhaps how you react in ways that obscure your real feelings.

This activity should be continued for at least four weeks with weekly review. If you continue to have trouble identifying your emotions, it might be helpful to consult a counselor or psychologist for professional input. Within several sessions, this person should be able to help you learn how to widen your repository and more effectively use all four emotion groups.

THINK ABOUT THIS TODAY

To laugh is to risk appearing a fool.
To weep is to risk appearing sentimental.
To reach out for another is to risk involvement.
To expose feelings is to risk exposing your true self.
To place your ideas, your dreams before the crowd is to risk their loss.
To love is to risk not being loved in return.
To live is to risk dying.
To hope is to risk despair.

To try is to risk failure.

> *But risks must be taken because the greatest hazard in life is to risk nothing. The person who risks nothing does nothing, has nothing, and is nothing. He may avoid suffering and sorrow, but he simply cannot learn, feel, change, grow, love, or live. Chained by his fears he is a slave. He is not free. Only a person who risks is free.*

> *Anonymous*

Words to Fathers:
Refer to the section entitled "How We Sidestep Our Feelings" and identify ways you may handle your emotions, especially uncomfortable ones. Then consciously practice using words related to the four emotions of mad, glad, sad, and scared instead of safe, intellectualized words like: "I think," "My opinion is," or "I believe."

Jesus expressed a wide range of emotions. He was amazed at the faith of the centurion, appreciative toward the woman who anointed him with oil, frustrated at the people's unbelief and lack of faith, tearful over the death of Lazarus, angry at the Pharisees, and in anguish over the anticipation of being crucified.

Read through the "Symptoms of Diminished Capacity for Emotional Intimacy in Men" and check as many as apply to you. Next, have your wife read through them and see if she checks the same ones or more of them. Wives usually identify twice as many of the symptoms in their husbands as do the men.

Suggestions for Sons:
Read through the Gospel of Matthew and underline each time Jesus expressed or experienced any emotion. Then make a list of the different ways He responded to various people and situations. Notice how versatile Jesus was and how appropriately He handled everyone's personal needs. Some people think of Jesus as primarily meek and mild,

but He was much more well-rounded than this. He responded with each emotion and in a healthy manner without sinning. How might you imitate His expression of feelings with your father?

Similarly, encourage the young men to be self-controlled. In everything set them an example by doing what is good. In your teaching show integrity, seriousness, and soundness of speech.

(Titus 2:6-8)

Dear Dad,

I know we haven't talked a lot over recent years like we used to about personal things. Lately, though, everything I am involved with is somehow coming apart at the seams. I have gotten myself in serious debt, my job has been affected by the recession, and Jenny and I are not getting along well. I hesitate to come crying on your shoulder, but I'm at a loss as to how to turn this all around. If you have any ideas, suggestions, or even prayers, I could sure use them about now. I hope you don't feel like I come to you only when I'm in trouble because I don't want to be a burden. If you get a chance, let me know what you think.

— twenty-nine-year-old man

SIX

The Mentor Method

"THE NEEDS AND WANTS of adults today are more important to them than those of their children." This was the consensus of a family conference held in November of 1989 in San José, California at the Stanford University Center for the Study of Families and Children. It appears that there has never been more attention or money directed toward adults and less for children. This group of scholars noted that the family-centered era has been waning for the last two decades in favor of the increasing self-centeredness of adults. This has been highlighted by the divorce rate of the last ten years, the average work week increasing from forty to approximately fifty-two hours, frequent moving for job promotions, and postponing or even deciding not to have children.[1] In short, it appears that more and more children are being left to fend for themselves while adults are out trying to find themselves, make their mark professionally, meet their goals, and get ahead.

More than ever our children need adults who will help them grow up. This involves walking through various developmental stages with them while giving guidance, feedback, support, and praise for their efforts. Sons particularly need a man whom they can admire, feel close to, be accepted by, observe, and learn from.

Many professions are very aware of the importance of the mentor method in training their up and coming candidates — medical schools, graduate schools, internship programs, blue collar apprenticeships, and assistant management positions to name only a few. The mentor method in father-son relationships requires one-on-one, man-to-man involvement in every facet of a son's development. There are so many times that a son needs his father to help him understand how to master different tasks in life. A few of these tasks include:

- learning how to swim
- throwing a baseball
- camping out
- standing up for oneself
- being friends with others
- treating females respectfully
- understanding the rules for different sports
- learning how to repair things around the house
- understanding what different professions involve
- developing confidence in themselves
- learning how to face their fears
- expressing feelings and needs openly.

Many of these learning experiences cannot be scheduled because children are not always receptive. They are open to learning in specific situations at the most unpredictable, not to mention inconvenient, times. Weekend fathers will often miss out on many of these opportunities. *Availability* is the key and *time* is the means through which the mentor method is accomplished. If we have neither the availability nor the time, our children will end up following someone else.

Just this summer alone both my boys have expressed interests in a number of activities which required me to stop, explain, and let them try to develop their skills in those areas. They asked to assist in mowing the grass, trimming the bushes, and helping me expand the deck in the backyard. It certainly would have been quicker for me to do it myself or let them try alone and later comment on their efforts, but we did these things together. They were able to ask questions and feel like they were contributing something to the family.

Recently they both also began playing football. While their mother and I were somewhat reluctant to encourage this interest due to the injuries I experienced when younger, we allowed it. Prior to their beginning, I spent time helping them learn how to sidestep tackles, catch the ball on the run, tackle low to bring an opponent down more easily, and run pass patterns that would fake out the defensive linebackers. This kind of one-on-one instruction may help them do well and avoid injuries. This is simply one example of the daily opportunities that fathers have to teach their sons when dads are available and willing to do so.

IDENTIFYING WITH DAD

Our children will identify with someone. Some of these occasions will be humorous, others heartwarming, and still others heartbreaking. One of my best high school buddies wrote me a letter recently describing a situation involving his young son with which many of us can identify:

Dear Chuck,
Annie and I had a wonderful time at the reunion visiting with everyone and seeing all our old classmates from years gone by. It's hard to believe we have been out of Wade Hampton High School for over twenty years.
Chuck, here's a humorous little piece of a father and son's special moment together I thought might interest you. One eve-

ning Annie, Clay, and I were watching a popular television talk show in which the host was interviewing a group of fathers who had raised their children only to discover later in life that they were not the true paternal fathers. Annie jokingly turned to me and asked, "What would you do if you found out you were not Clay's father?" In response I turned to Clay and asked, "Who's your daddy?" Clay quickly remarked, "Uncle Jack." I looked at Annie in total shock and then we both laughed out loud. I knew he was fond of his Uncle Jack but this was ridiculous.

> *Sincerely,*
> *Billy*

Many of us have had the funny experience of having our child point to a total stranger in the mall or grocery store and say, "Daddy!" There seems to be an instinctive desire within each of us to identify with someone. Our children are particularly susceptible to this in the early years. As fathers, the time to establish a deep and lasting relationship with our sons is when they are young. Sadly, many fathers ignore their sons until their later teenage years and then, realizing their mistake, attempt to cultivate a relationship that their sons are no longer interested in. These lost opportunities plague fathers and adversely affect sons for the rest of their lives if not resolved.

Psalm 128:3 explains one result of the father who fears the Lord: "Your sons will be like olive shoots around your table." This passage describes the rich opportunities we have to cultivate the health and well-being of our sons from the very beginning. Olive shoots are green, tender, and vulnerable. They need protection, nourishment, and guidance. To the Jewish people the olive tree was the emblem of prosperity, blessing, deity, and strength. The olive tree thrives best in warm and sunny conditions. It grows slowly and lives many years looking very vigorous. Much like these olive shoots, our sons need our consistent involvement as fathers. Parenting is not just an obligation and responsibility. It is an opportunity because fathers frequently benefit and grow as much as their children do in this process of parenting. Sons identify with and imitate their fathers more when they are directly involved with each other. It is not enough to tell them what to do or for them to watch us do it. We must participate together. Remember the old maxim, "If you hear, you forget. If you see, you remember. If you do, you understand."

TWO KINDS OF MALE MENTORS

"You then, my son, be strong in the grace that is in Christ Jesus. And the things you have heard me say in the presence of many witnesses entrust to reliable men who will also be qualified to teach others" (2 Tim. 2:1-2). Fathers teach their sons by example or default. It is impossible as a father to not be an influence for better or worse upon our sons. Fathers who care what their sons think of them and who try to be a positive influence commonly provide two models. These two might be best described as the *admired father* and the *involved influence*.

The *admired father* is looked up to by his son. Dad is viewed as his hero. His son may walk, talk, and want to be like Dad when he grows up. His father is better than any father at everything he does. Whatever he says must be the truth and whatever he does has to be the best in the eyes of the idealistic son. Who wouldn't envy a father who was thought of as highly by his son as this. Don't we all want to be seen as the best dad in the world?

Upon closer examination, however, this father-son relationship may not be as great as one would assume. The father may be projecting an idealized image to which his son could never hope to measure up. If this type of image is established early in the formative years of a child, when he becomes a teenager he may be in for quite a disappointment. Fathers who are too invested in maintaining a position of admiration often do not allow their sons the opportunity to know the real person beneath the image. A father may not talk about his fears or weaknesses. So when they become apparent in later years, a son may feel surprised if not betrayed. This is especially likely to occur if a father insists on maintaining his position of _super dad_.

I know one father who is particularly impressive in business, sports, society, and finances. His son has tried to imitate him in many of those areas. However, this father has never really allowed his son to get emotionally close to him and know the real person behind the accomplishments. Now this son resents his dad instead of admiring him and has caused his family a great deal of grief through his misbehavior and antagonistic conduct. Since he is older, he sees his father's shortcomings more clearly and it angers him. However, he still wants his father's acceptance, but because of the damage done that dream of closeness may never be fully realized.

It is not enough for a father to be admired or to maintain a pedestal-perfect image in the eyes of his son. He must be real, acknowledge his fears and faults, and let his son see him struggle with life and its difficulties. Fathers cannot afford to act like their human frailties do not exist. Perhaps one of the best examples of the _admired father_ was immortalized in Harry Chapin's song, "Cat's in the Cradle." The son wanted to be just like his dad, yet was never close to him because the time was not provided. The son did, in fact, become like his dad. However, he was no more involved with his children than was his father.

The _involved influence_ father may not be placed on a pedestal or seen as the infallible hero by his son; however, he is the essence of masculinity. His emotional availability allows his son the opportunity to understand the person he is. His son knows he is not perfect, yet the gift Dad provides is an example of one who is determined to face his fears and learn from his mistakes.

Fathers who are _involved influences_ frequently benefit and grow emotionally as much as their children do. This provides an atmosphere in which fathers and sons become friends. This type of father is real in that he does not mind sharing his specific daily struggles. This accessibility allows his son to learn firsthand how to face life one day at a time. This father helps his son take mistakes and setbacks and turn them into a "lesson learned" for the future. He teaches his son to be the best person he can be. When a father helps his son find a purpose, a worthy cause, or a reason for being alive that son develops direction and meaning for himself. In this sense, a father may even model faith for his son. Children who are able to find this purpose and a set of values by which to live are much less likely to use drugs or engage in self-destructive behavior.

In the song, "Leader of the Band," Dan Fogelberg writes about his relationship with his father. He sings about how he has tried to imitate his father and how he hopes to be seen as a "living legacy." The fathers who are *involved influences* with their sons may not maintain high visibility in the community. They may not have admirable business reputations. Often, these fathers have opted to commit their time and energies to an even greater cause, their wives and families. It is there where their legacy lies.

When we are on our deathbeds and we look back upon what we have accomplished, will we have wished we had earned more money, worked longer hours, or received greater promotions? Or, will we have wished we had spent more time with the people we loved—our sons, daughters, wives, family, and friends?

MY THREE MENTORS

Every boy needs a mentor to help him learn to become a man. It is an impossible job for a youngster to do on his own. There is something within that causes each of us to look for a hero, an example, or a model to follow. It gives us a frame of reference, a measuring stick, or a goal toward which we can strive.

My first mentor was my father. I always admired his courage in leaving his family, friends, and surroundings in the Philadelphia area and moving deep into the South with his wife and children to take a job. My father was a hard worker who was determined and persistent. Although he only had a high school education and some college courses, through hard work he eventually secured an executive position with a large, international company during the thirty-five years he worked for them.

I have always admired my father's character, integrity, and honesty. Above all, he taught me to tell the truth. Early in life he equipped me with the skills to play sports and defend myself. This instilled a confidence in me which I have relied upon throughout my life. My father has a deep but quiet faith. While he did not express his feelings well as I grew up, I sensed how strongly he experienced things within himself. During our earlier years he rarely expressed his love for me, but I always knew that he cared. Later in life I began telling him that I loved him and it took him almost ten years to be able to say the words back to me. I never doubted his love for me, but felt that for his sake and mine these words ("I love you") should be expressed. And now we do. Since he has retired we have become computer buddies. We call each other and share the latest programs or tidbits of computer information we have discovered. My dad has given me a great deal. He taught me to never give up, to face my fears, to work hard, and to be honest and truthful.

My next mentor was Chuck. He was several years older than me, and I met him while in graduate school at the University of Florida. He was an incredibly intuitive, bright young man who had perhaps the most capable leadership abilities I had ever seen. He was a great judge of character. His ability to bring out the best in the people around him was without equal. While Chuck was a strong personality, he was also extremely expressive. He was able to help people have a vision for themselves that might have otherwise gone undeveloped. Chuck gave me opportunities to develop myself musically, spiritually, professionally, and personally. His passion for Jesus Christ and winning others to the Lord was without equal. I had never met anyone like him. His organizational abilities allowed him to command large groups of people and cultivate team unity that could accomplish a great deal. Chuck is still a great friend of mine. He helped me to believe in myself; build my confidence; act on my faith in God; strive for excellence; and to express my love, affection, and gratitude openly.

My next mentor is not a man, but my wife. From the first time I met her, I knew that she was an enthusiastic, exciting, high-energy person. She also was extremely intuitive and very bright. We met at Clemson University. I was particularly impressed with how determined she was to do the best she could in whatever she pursued. Her attention to detail, ability to apply herself, and sense of responsibility made me admire her greatly. She was the single most important factor in improving my GPA in college from a 1.7 to a 3.4 in two years. I have always appreciated her personal willingness to sacrifice for others. She has quite an ability to make other people feel loved. Her loyalty to her friends is exceptional. Her sensitivity to the needs of our children has often made me feel she should have the degree in psychology. My wife has truly helped me realize that being a man means becoming emotionally available, responsive, and sensitive to the needs of others. She has helped me trust my intuitions and recognize the power of their accuracy. She has helped me also to become "tuned in" to the needs of our two sons.

We should never underestimate the positive influence we can have on another person. There are numerous occasions in our son's life where we can make a difference in the direction he takes. These potential turning points are ever present yet it takes an alert, involved, and persistent parent to capitalize on these opportunities.

SEVEN LESSONS A FATHER CAN TEACH HIS SON

I recall reading an article describing a father and his young son discovering the value of teamwork in attempting to climb Mount Kilimanjaro, the highest mountain on the African continent. The five days they spent ascending the over 19,000-foot mountain taught them some very meaningful lessons about life. It was a great opportunity for both a father and his eight-year-old son to experience hardships together. Each saw how the other handled these difficulties from their perspectives—one an adult and the other a child.[2]

The entire journey emphasized the importance of *taking life one step at a time*. It is quite a temptation in our society to expect quick success with minimal effort. While perseverance and stamina are necessary if anyone is to accomplish the more difficult goals of life, no one can develop such attributes without personal sacrifice. By following through with our commitments, we learn to appreciate the value of putting one foot in front of the other.

My oldest son has a tendency to give up if a task seems difficult, much like I did when I was younger. By patiently helping him try a little harder for a little while longer, he has succeeded where he might have previously given up. He is slowly but surely changing that tendency in his life.

On the other hand, my youngest son has an inherent sense of determination that causes him to stick with a task until it is mastered. I remember one occasion when he was a four-year-old watching some boys play basketball. Later he stood alone with the ball throwing it toward the rim for one hour until he finally put the ball through the hoop.

Another important lesson a father can teach his son is *teamwork*. The all too prevalent American attitude of individualism causes people to do things by themselves in their own way. Such an outlook, however, denies the fact that we all need help sometimes. There will always be times when we need another to get us through a difficult situation. American men find it difficult to ask for help because they do not want to appear weak or incompetent. But, it is a strength to trust and depend on another individual. I tend to do most things on my own without getting input or assistance. While this enables me to do things my way and enjoy the satisfaction of having done it all, it also causes me to make unnecessary mistakes and to miss out on other ways of solving the problem. This can be a very embarrassing and often costly mistake. I have learned, albeit slowly, over the years to take my time, get others' points of view, and be ready to change my approach if it is necessary. By sharing our needs and helping one another, we can encourage others to excel beyond their own limited expectations of themselves. "United we stand; divided we fall." "A cord of three strands is not quickly broken" (Ecc. 4:12).

Thirdly, *life is difficult.* Problems and unexpected circumstances inevitably descend upon us all. However, we can prepare for these tough times by developing and deepening our spiritual resources.

In my youngest son's soccer league is a boy who was born with a deformed arm. It is much smaller than his other arm and virtually useless. I sympathize with families who have these unfortunate circumstances befall them. As a psychologist, I know the emotional hardships these children will have to face. What is particularly encouraging about this situation is how little this disability seems to affect the young man. He seems to make friends easily and interact with others uninhibitedly. In fact, he is an excellent athlete and as aggressive a competitor as I have seen. He is quite impressive! Someone apparently has taken the time in this young boy's life to help him compensate for his misfortune. That son is well on his way to realizing that life may be difficult but it is possible.

Our sons need to see us turning to Jesus Christ, calling upon His strength and guidance at all times—good as well as bad. Our sons should see this depth of faith in us so that they can learn to imitate it. It is our responsibility as Christian fathers to disciple our sons in formal as well as informal ways.

The fourth lesson to learn is *how to accept disappointment.* Disappointment comes into all of our lives in various forms and at different times beginning when we are quite young. While it is essential that our sons experience success in order to encourage them to persevere, they must also learn how to handle defeat. No one wins all the time. There is something good that can come out of every unfortunate setback. For Christians every situation has an upside, a bright spot, or a redeeming aspect if we simply look for it. "In all things God works for the good of those who love Him, who have been called according to His purpose" (Rom. 8:28). I try not to use the word *failure* and replace it instead with *lesson.* "What lessons did you learn from this experience?" "How would you do it differently next time?" "How are you better off having gone through this?" These are all good questions for helping our sons redeem the disappointments they face.

Fifthly, *endurance is a necessary ingredient if we are to succeed in life.* Many people never realize that victory is not primarily reserved for those who are the smartest, strongest, luckiest, or best looking, but for those who endure. This lesson was proven to me time and time again in school. I'm an individual with only average intelligence, so it has been more difficult for me to achieve my goals. I can remember having to work harder and longer than most of my friends to just get by in school, while they appeared to do well with little effort. At the time it seemed unfair to me that I had to work so hard for so little.

In retrospect, I realize by enduring and persevering that anyone can reach their goals in life. There are many bright, talented, and capable people who give up because they do not want to expend the effort that it takes to accomplish their objectives. Scripture gives us this exhortation, "Blessed is the man who perseveres under trial, because when he has stood the test, he will receive the crown of life that God has promised to those who love Him" (James 1:12).

The next lesson that a father can teach his son is to *do your best*. Because we are not perfect, we need only do our best. Theodore Roosevelt once said, "Do what you can with what you have where you are." One of the greatest mistakes we can make is to compare ourselves with others. There will always be someone who does better or worse. Using such a yardstick can cause us to feel superior or inferior—neither of which meets biblical expectations. However, when we compete against ourselves we always win if we have tried our best. We can always improve upon our own performance. This way we can feel good about ourselves and celebrate the achievements of others without feeling envious or discouraged.

Finally, *take time to enjoy your achievements*. Celebrate your success. We all deserve credit for a job well done. Take time to reflect upon the journey and how your goals were met. Our fast-paced society coupled with our deep-seated insecurities cause us to finish one project and quickly move to another as if to say, "I'm still not good enough." Make time to savor life's successes. It is important for our sons to celebrate each of their milestones. All along, however, we must be reiterating that the person they *are* is more important than the things they *do*.

Dads, our kids will learn from someone. They will look for direction and meaning in their lives. If we do not provide the input and influence, someone else will. Often the choices our young, inexperienced sons make are not influences of which we would approve. There are no short cuts to helping our sons become the kind of Christian men they have the potential to be. There are costs: time, attention, patience, money, and effort. The rewards, however, are worth it. As John stated it so aptly, "I have no greater joy than to hear that my children are walking in the truth" (3 John 4). The choice is ours today, it will be our son's choice tomorrow.

Words to Fathers:
Go back and review the section entitled "Seven Lessons a Father Can Teach His Son." What are some specific ways you could help your son learn these lessons of life? Try to think of practical situations where you could apply the principles of: taking life one step at a time; fostering teamwork; accepting difficulties as part of life; accepting disappointments as lessons; enduring until you succeed; doing your best; and taking time to enjoy accomplishments.

Suggestions for Sons:
Who were your mentors when you were growing up? Make a mental list of all the things you learned from them that helped you develop. Call or write them and express your appreciation for their interest in you. Do you currently have a mentor? We all need someone we can go to for direction personally, spiritually, or professionally at various times of need in our lives. Who would you want to fill this role for you?

For God did not give us a spirit of timidity, but a spirit of power, of love, and of self-discipline.

(2 Tim. 1:7)

My father made me work so hard as a kid, I was determined to not expect much from my son. Now, he is so irresponsible I don't know what to do. We have spent thousands of dollars just bailing him out of one problem after another.
—fifty-year-old corporate executive

SEVEN

Cultivating Courage, Developing Determination, and Promoting Perseverance

COURAGE, DETERMINATION, AND PERSEVERANCE are qualities of character that are still illusive to many adults in our generation. To stand up for what we believe in, act on a decision toward a purpose, and to steadily persist in a course of action requires a great deal of discipline and maturity. How is a son to learn such difficult but necessary lessons? It is not easy in today's society.

Today's children are constantly exposed to the philosophy that "life should be fair, painless, and comfortable." This may be a reasonable expectation for youngsters, but as children develop they need to learn to live with the reality of life in a fallen world.

Sons, old enough to have regular playmates, often complain when faced with conflict, "That's not fair!" Shortly thereafter we are visited with their tearful requests to resolve the inequitable dilemma between them. As fathers we may be able to urge our sons to take turns, insure equity between what each child receives, and to teach them to share, but ultimately a difficult problem will enter their lives. Reality teaches us that *life is not fair*. If our children grow up believing injustices should not occur to them, they will be very frustrated individuals. Life doles out its share of unfortunate circumstances to us all. How we react to these shapes our destiny.

We are also subjected to daily advertisements which tell us "pain and suffering should be avoided at all costs." There is supposedly a pill, cure, remedy, or treatment for anything that ails us nowadays. While we may not realize it, this philosophy inadvertently encourages a great deal of the substance abuse that occurs in our society today. Instead of facing problems, we anesthetize ourselves to avoid their pain. By quickly medicating the pain we are experiencing, we cheat ourselves of the opportunity to learn to deal with life's difficult dilemmas.

The final fallacious philosophy that our society promotes is that, "life should be comfortable." Many of us seem engaged in full-time endeavors to create comfortable lives for ourselves. We highly support an upwardly-mobile mentality in our country, with the goal of increasing the standard of living and quality of our lives. We are constantly buying bigger and better homes, cars, furniture, and electronic equipment. Retirement funds and annuity accounts abound in hopes that someday we might enjoy the good life during our final years.

However, an interesting phenomena occurs in the middle and older generations as they become more financially self-sufficient. As their "comfort zone" becomes established, they seem to withdraw from regular contact with other people. As they acquire goods and amass monies, they no longer seem to need others. The result is a subtle trick that our materialistic focus plays on them. They quit taking risks, reaching out, and testing the limits of their capabilities. In short, they simply stop growing emotionally. I believe this is one major reason why the older generation gets so "set in its ways" and becomes pessimistic.

This is the curse of the older generations, but it's not too late to protect the youth of today. What should we do about these insidiously damaging philosophies which threaten to indoctrinate our children? First of all, we should help them see that while life may not always be fair, it is manageable. God gave us each the freedom of choice, and with that blessing also came a limitation. We are not perfect people and therefore will make mistakes. When we exercise our freedom of choice we will occasionally, although unintentionally, hurt other people. All of us have made decisions that we thought were initially correct only to later find out that they caused someone else a problem. While this is unfortunate indeed, especially if we are on the receiving end of the injustice, it often can be resolved and worked out. Learning from the mistakes we make is an important part of adapting to life. Looking for the good that results from a bad situation will help us maintain a sense of optimism and hope about the future.

Pain also is a part of life. Tennyson once wrote, "Tis better to have loved and lost, than never to have loved at all." He was addressing the need for risk-taking to make our lives more meaningful. However, with these risks also come painful experiences. Suffering is part of the human condition. Anyone whose first consideration is how much suffering, sacrifice, or pain an upcoming situation might cause them, will become an extremely cautious, inhibited individual who misses out on much of life's excitement. While we do not want our children to live with reckless abandon, we also do not want them to be paralyzed by their fears. It is the risks a man takes that make him great.

We should all strive to expand our "comfort zones." By pushing ourselves past the point of comfort, we grow emotionally. This enables us to continually face our fears. When challenges are avoided and conflicts ignored, our insecurities creep in and paralyze us. We need goals in our lives to keep us developing as individuals. When we retire from active involvement in life, we become doubtful, unsure, and self-conscious. It is actually a blessing that life is unfair and uncomfortable, because it keeps us in tune with what our needs are as people, as well as the needs of others around us. It provides us with a means of evolving as people from birth through death, and a chance to realize the potential that God gave us during our short stay on earth.

CULTIVATING COURAGE

Fathering isn't for cowards. Sons need to be shown a model of a man who is facing his fears and overcoming them. Men often behave by never acknowledging their fears, hoping this example will somehow help their sons to be courageous. Denying we are afraid cheats our sons out of the opportunity to see that fear is a normal part of life. How we face it is the key to cultivating courage.

At the 1989 Annual American Association for Marriage and Family Therapy Conference in San Francisco, several well-known family therapists affirmed that fathers should take a "heroic journey" into themselves to face their feelings of fear. They stated that the more men are comfortable with all of their emotions including anger, sadness, and joy, the more freely they can honestly share themselves with others. Men can learn from other men what their personal issues are and how to deal with them. One of the presenters advocated the involvement of strong, nurturing fathers to be present and available on a daily basis for their children. He noted that such involvement could change the course of history in the developing of boys into men.[1]

There are a variety of ways by which men begin cultivating courage in their sons. One is by helping them realize that *life is a series of lessons.* The good and bad that happen to us are merely examples of being enrolled in a full-time informal school called life. Each day we have opportunity to learn lessons that will help us grow up. We may like the lessons or think them irrelevant or foolish. Some of these lessons will cause pain and tempt us to avoid them. Our job as fathers is to help our sons focus on the goal and not the pain. Pain is a part of everyday life. When understood properly, it can become a means to developing determination for reaching our goals.

When I was in high school and learning to play the guitar and sing, it was initially terrifying to get up in front of an audience. My anxiety hampered my performance, adding insult to injury. However, to improve and learn to perform professionally, it was necessary to subject myself to these uncomfortable circumstances. Fortunately, after a number of exposures, I was able to look forward to performing for others. I also realized that a certain amount of apprehensiveness actually improved the quality of my performance because it acted as a motivator to help me want to do my best, and therefore, practice and prepare more for these performances.

The second principle that fathers can teach their children is that _there are no mistakes, only lessons._ Growth is a process of experimentation: trial and error. The errors are as much a part of the process of learning as the successes are.

I was very impressed with the coaches for the Norcross, Georgia Dixie Youth Baseball League this past spring. Their motto is to "praise every effort." As long as a child is trying, he is succeeding. They even congratulated strikeouts as long as the player was swinging his bat. No error was criticized as long as the child was trying.

We need to encourage our sons to be willing to try and then we should praise any effort. By encouraging them to "do their best" while not expecting perfection, we allow them to compete against their own best performance. This saves them from comparing themselves with others. We have encouraged our sons to be one of the first in their classes to contribute to a discussion. This encourages them to be a part of the process, to consider what they can offer to the group, and allows them to take a risk on their own.

The third lesson a father must teach his son is to *face his fears*. James Baldwin once said that, "Not everything that is faced can be changed, but nothing can be changed until it is faced." In our society today, we spend a great deal of time ignoring problems, avoiding conflict, or engaging in the "paralysis by analysis." Obviously no situation can be solved if it is not faced. However, sometimes we talk a problem to death and never act on our solution. Knowing all the answers is great, but worthless if you do not act upon them. Nike has coined an appropriate advertising slogan that sums it up: "Just do it."

It is imperative to be equipped with the skills to solve life's problems. In our teens, twenties, and thirties, we seem to hone these skills to a finer degree. However, in our forties and fifties, an interesting phenomenon seems to occur. We develop ways to insulate our lives, categorize our priorities, focus on our strengths, often ignoring our weaknesses and areas of discomfort. Ultimately we find ourselves having gone full circle and standing face-to-face with many of the childhood fears that we have ignored during our later adult years. But, if we expect our sons to face their fears throughout their lives, we as fathers must do the same. This requires developing a determination toward life that will nurture our sons in courage.

DEVELOPING DETERMINATION

One of the things that I always admired about my middle brother, Hank, is his determination. He is a hard worker who will stay with a job until it is finished. I believe he must have inherited that tendency from our father who is very much the same way.

Determination is acting on a decision to succeed at a purpose, no matter the cost or time involved. All of us have started out with the intention of accomplishing something, only to become distracted or discouraged because of the setbacks we encountered. Fathers can help their sons realize that there are lessons in the setbacks. In fact, the Lord seems to repeat lessons in our lives until they are learned. It is very easy to give up when we don't initially succeed and then go on to something else. However, we eventually find ourselves faced with a situation that resembles that lesson we still need to learn.

One of the most practical ways we see this lesson repeated is in the area of our finances. If we have not learned to live within our budget, we will become overextended time and time again. People who are constantly late will find themselves left behind or left out. Halfhearted efforts also show a lack of determination.

I am one of those individuals who has an average amount of ability. To succeed at anything, I must give a 100 percent effort. This is true for me in academics, sports, relationships, and my spiritual life. I used to admire individuals who were bright and talented enough to show an above-average performance with a below-average effort. I now realize that most of those people never reached their potential or fully appreciated their accomplishments.

One reminder that I have had to give over and over to my sons has been to *be patient with yourself when you are learning new things.* There is something in all of us that wants to be an expert yesterday. We want to give a minimal effort and receive a maximum output. This seems to be one lesson that Ken, my youngest brother, has learned better than the rest of us. He tends to take his time and pace himself well. I, on the other hand, have always been an impatient learner and now find myself having to deal with my oldest son's impatience with himself. It is important to remind him that we all have positive and negative capabilities and what we focus on is what we give strength to. Helping our sons find their strengths as well as setting realistic goals insures their success.

When Chris was learning to play soccer, he was once criticized by his peers. He wanted to quit and just watch the other guys play, but we encouraged him to get back in the game and try again. We talked to him about not letting someone else's criticism stop him from reaching his own goals. Kids tend to compare themselves with others and become discouraged, rather than recognizing they can only do the best they can. Chris was able to get back into the game with a renewed determination to play his hardest. This is the sort of everyday attitude we need to instill in our sons.

PROMOTING PERSEVERANCE

Perseverance means persisting with a goal until it is reached. Life is difficult, but it is possible. The late Winston Churchill once gave a famous seven word speech, admonishing his audience to, "Never, never, never, never, never give up."

Fathers need to teach their sons to take one day at a time. This is a popular phrase that Alcoholics Anonymous uses to help its members continue in their program of sobriety. When I started school at Clemson University I wondered how I would be able to finish four years of classes and exams. I eventually realized I had to take one class at a time and before long, a week, a month, and a semester had passed. Time management specialists use the "Swiss cheese approach" to poke holes in a large project by doing a portion at a time so that it will not seem so overwhelming. When jogging once with my youngest son, David, he quickly tired and wanted to return home. By asking him to run just one more block with me before he went home, he was able to extend his endurance to complete the entire run around the neighborhood.

Children and adults need to realize that today is all we have been guaranteed. We need to focus on the present, concentrate all our energies in accomplishing the task at hand. Too many people either live in the past of old achievements or the future of how things will be when. . . . When we are able to focus on one goal at a time we can experience the full benefit of the moment. It is difficult in our fast-paced society to learn contentment by just doing one thing at a time.

Finally, our sons will continue to embrace life enthusiastically if we can help them realize that *learning lessons does not end.* There is no part of life that does not provide us lessons. If we are alive, there are lessons to be learned. I remember in graduate school one of the major goals was to help us become students of life, to continually ask questions and seek answers. The more we know, the more we realize we need to learn.

The goal of cultivating courage, developing determination, and promoting perseverance is maturity. One mark of mature adults is the ability to take care of our families and prepare our sons to take care of their future ones.

Words to Fathers:
Write your son a letter about how proud you are of him. Let him know specific areas where you've seen his courage growing in the lessons he has learned from his mistakes. Congratulate him on how he faces his fears. Praise him for his determination in the goals he has set for himself. Help him feel your support by persevering in difficult situations. Remind him how you and God are his greatest cheering section and that you both will always be there for him.

Suggestions for Sons:
Write your dad a letter about how proud and grateful you are for him. Let him know specific reasons why you admire and respect him. Identify ways he has helped you learn how to handle life's difficulties. Thank him for the ways he has been an example, mentor, or even hero for you in helping you face life's fears.

*Make every effort to add to your faith goodness; and to good-
ness, knowledge; and to knowledge, self-control; and to self-
control, perseverance; and to perseverance, godliness; and
to godliness, brotherly kindness; and to brotherly kindness,
love. For if you possess these qualities in increasing measure,
they will keep you from being ineffective and unproductive
in your knowledge of our Lord Jesus Christ.*

(2 Peter 1:5-8)

*My father really knows the Bible. He is ready to help other
people in need at any time. He is also an endless resource of
advice on any topic. However, I really don't know the man
on the inside and he doesn't really know me. I admire him
but I don't like him because he has kept the most important
part of himself from me — who he is.*

— twenty-eight-year-old man

*My dad helped me out a lot during a tough time last year. He
helped me like myself when I didn't feel anyone else did. He
reminded me that God has always loved me. We did a lot of
things together. He also let me do things with my friends.
He's a good dad.*

— twelve-year-old boy

EIGHT

Developing Spiritual Leadership and a Passion for Christ

HISTORY SHOWS US that there are no limits to the effects that one individual can have in shaping the lives of many. Jesus Christ is the most outstanding example of this. Unfortunately, in the area of spiritual development most men have taken a backseat within the family. Nowadays the woman is primarily recognized as the spiritually oriented parent. Fathers may attend church regularly with their families, giving the appearance of spiritual leadership; but with the exception of their involvement in jobs and hobbies, most men are interested in little else. Sure they can show interest and enthusiasm about their latest acquisition or sizable investment profit, but spiritual concerns rarely generate their interest.

However, without an active faith, we gradually become apathetic toward other areas in life. Only a spiritual purpose can insure enduring hope and direction. One person with a belief is equal to ninety-nine with only interest. While a wife and mother can and does instill deep spiritual values within her son, a father's genuine and active faith adds a spiritual dimension that profoundly affects a son. However, a father cannot pass on something he does not possess. Each man must have his own personal relationship to God. As fathers, we can encourage our sons by modeling a sincere relationship with Jesus Christ that consciously affects the lives of others for the kingdom.

IS YOUR HEART TOTALLY COMMITTED TO CHRIST?

Father, ask your son, "What do you think is most important in my life?" and listen for his response. If he says anything other than, "Loving God," you may have a serious spiritual problem with which to contend. Our children know what is most important to us. They see what we spend our time doing and what excites us. They will imitate that example. Do we have the attitude of David, "As the deer pants for streams of water, so my soul pants for You, O God. My soul thirsts for God, for the living God. When can I go and meet with God?" (Ps. 42:1-2)

Recently, my youngest son, David, amazed me with his spiritual focus and awareness. I was teaching his class in Sunday School and during a puppet show, one of the puppets asked the children, "How was your Christmas?" To this, one of the children yelled out, "Boring!" In response to this David replied, "Do you think the birth of Jesus was boring?" I was very impressed by his passion for Christ.

Sons should regularly see their fathers studying the Bible and praying. A father who begins his day this way makes a strong impression upon his young son.

Parents have a tremendous opportunity to participate in the Bible reading and prayer time of their children at bedtime. It gives children an opportunity to hear us talk with God and learn about prayer. And listening to their prayers helps us know what's on their minds and how their concepts of God are developing.

Another important time for children is Sunday morning during preparation for church. Too many families argue, fuss, and complain until they reach the church building, and then after services are over, resume life forgetting to apply anything they may have learned.

Fathers who do not talk about spiritual things or who attend church because they are supposed to, are inadvertently teaching their children that Christianity is a responsibility and obligation that one must meet, much like other duties in one's life. When our sons hear us talking about spiritual applications, issues we are struggling with, our love and concern for other people becoming Christians, they realize we are serious about our relationship to God. When we share our homes and our faith with other friends and neighbors, they understand that our purpose on earth is to help others develop and nurture a relationship with Christ. Fathers who are not actively modeling their faith, but who opt to be good examples by being nice guys, will not influence their sons to spread the Gospel to others.

DO YOU HAVE THE ATTITUDE OF A DISCIPLE?

What is the attitude of a disciple of Jesus Christ? Is it like the line from the old Frank Sinatra song, "I did it my way" or is it similar to the popular male philosophy of today: self-sufficiency and rugged independence? It is actually captured in the psalmist's words, "Search me, O God, and know my heart; test me and know my anxious thoughts. See if there is any offensive way in me, and lead me in the way everlasting" (Ps. 139:23-24).

The disciple's attitude is one of humility and receptiveness. The heart of a disciple says, "I can learn from anyone and I am willing to change if need be." The Lord wants us to be mature, determined, and filled with conviction. Yet He also wants us to be willing to adjust our position when His Word indicates otherwise: "I will instruct you and teach you in the way you should go; I will counsel you and watch over you. Do not be like the horse or the mule, which have no understanding but must be controlled by bit and bridle or they will not come to you. Many are the woes of the wicked, but the LORD's unfailing love surrounds the man who trusts in Him" (Ps. 32:8-10).

There is a certain closed-mindedness that comes with age. As mature adults we often think we have seen all that life has to offer. It is hard to believe that there is anything new under the sun. In fact, those of us raised in Christian homes often believe that by the time we have attended Sunday School or church a few hundred times, we know all there could be about God. And so we begin to maintain a "holding pattern" in our minds about who God is. It is as if we know everything about God and will have to wait until death to find out the rest. This shallow understanding causes men to get distracted by other things, anesthetizing their spiritual sensitivity and enthusiasm toward Jesus Christ.

Fathers who have a neutral attitude toward spiritual things do more harm to their sons' future relationships with God than they know. Fathers who are enthusiastic, disciplined, and believe that their committed Christian example can make a difference, will provide a rich spiritual legacy for their sons' futures.

DO YOU LEAD WITH A SERVANT ATTITUDE?

Our world is governed by spiritual paradoxes. The person who takes time to help others is much more fulfilled than one who merely looks out for "number one." The individual who is willing to give of his resources surprisingly finds himself blessed in more ways than ever imagined. The individual who is willing to give his life for a cause greater than himself is truly able to enjoy life. Likewise, the person who is constantly protecting himself feels very little security about the future.

Effective leaders are not successful because they drive people or demand total compliance, but because they lead others by example and willingness to sacrifice. Integrity is the willingness to make sacrifices for what we believe to be true. People are more than willing to follow a person of integrity. In your family, are you the first to apologize if you have made a mistake? We are often unwilling to change unless someone else changes first. Fathers who expect their sons to follow them must lead by showing this kind of example of humility.

Consider the following questions. Do you reflect a servant attitude when faced with these family situations?

- Are you thoughtful and sensitive to the needs of other family members?
- Will you inconvenience yourself to help your wife around the house?
- Will you do jobs together so you can spend time with your sons?
- Do you remember important events like his games, plays, or parent/teacher meetings?
- Are you there when you say you will be for your son?
- Are you willing to have your son's friends in your homes for visits or overnight stays, even if it's inconvenient or interrupts your routine?
- Are you positive in looking for the best in your friends and neighbors, even if it would be easier to go along with the criticisms they might be receiving?
- When you are tired and worn out, are you irritable, harsh, and impatient?
- Can you temporarily put aside your own needs and attend to your son's concerns?

How did you measure up? If you're discouraged remember Jesus' standard, "Whoever wants to become great among you must be your servant, and whoever wants to be first must be your slave—just as the Son of Man did not come to be served, but to serve, and to give His life as a ransom for many" (Matt. 20:26-28).

DO YOU HAVE A MATURING FAITH IN CHRIST?

Most men spend a great portion of their lives trying to prove they are competent, capable, strong, worthwhile, and equal to other men. If the truth be known, most of us spend the first half of our lives trying to prove that we "have what it takes" and the second half of our lives trying to prove "we haven't lost it." Most men will not openly admit that these fears exist. However, comparing ourselves to others can have an eroding effect upon our faith in God and our trust in one another. We become so afraid of being hurt or taken advantage of that we remain aloof and detached from close friendships or strong commitments. This can be devastating to our spiritual lives because we begin to believe if we do not take care of ourselves, no one will. But when we go through tough times, God is there waiting to supply what we lack if we believe and give Him the chance.

Each of our lives is a story of faith. As we look back on them, we see opportunities where God has transformed our weaknesses into strengths. Paul's testimony rings true, "I can do all things through Him who strengthens me" (Phil. 4:13, NASB). As I look back at my life I'm grateful for the times I relied on God. But there are also those times in which I depended on myself. During the former times, I was less in control, could not see the outcome, and yet in retrospect see how God was using me. In the latter times, I was more in control, but more insecure, and the outcomes left me with more regrets.

I remember my first job search after graduate school. I wanted to work in a mental health center so that I could acquire the experience to enter private practice. I was a relatively young Christian, still growing in my faith, who frankly needed to continue my association with my local church because of all the spiritual influence I was receiving. I interviewed for three different jobs, two of which were out of town. The third job was located in the town where I lived, but it was the least desirable to me. I was very fortunate to have been offered all three jobs simultaneously; however, that placed me in a very difficult dilemma: Do I choose a job based on what I think would more quickly enhance my professional development? Or do I choose the job that would allow me to remain in the church that had helped me grow spiritually?

After a great deal of prayer, counsel, and consideration, I chose the job that would afford me the greatest enrichment spiritually. Within two years, several interesting developments occurred at the other positions I had declined. One facility actually closed its doors within a year, and the second one came under legal scrutiny for mishandling government funds. In effect, had I chosen either of the other two jobs, despite their apparent professional advantages, I would probably have been unemployed or unhappy.

Ironically, the least desirable job afforded me a great deal of very valuable experience. I was promoted to an Assistant Director position under a psychiatrist who later began a private practice and offered me the use of his facility at no charge. Eventually, the experience I had acquired in this first position made me the top candidate for a job that opened in the mental health system of the town where I had remained. Only God could have foreseen that I would be offered this position if I just demonstrated patience, faith, and keeping Him first in my life. The author of Hebrews says it well, "Now faith is being sure of what we hope for and certain of what we do not see" (Heb. 11:1).

DO YOU SHARE YOUR FAITH WITH OTHERS?

As men, perhaps the greatest test of our faith is whether or not we share it, or better yet, whether we have anything to share. It is uncommon for men to have conversations with other men about spiritual matters. We may talk with members of our church, but to approach a friend or a business associate and strike up a spiritual conversation is a rarity indeed.

If you were asked to go out today and talk about what Jesus Christ means to you to another man, could you do it? Would you have feelings of anxiety and inadequacy worrying about what others would think of you? What would your purpose and goal of the conversation be? How would you begin it? Do you really believe God wants you to talk with others about who He is? You might ask, "Why is that my job to do this? Hasn't it already been done?"

The last thing Matthew records Jesus saying was, "All authority in heaven and on earth has been given to Me. Therefore go and make disciples of all nations, baptizing them in the name of the Father and the Son and the Holy Spirit, and teaching them to obey everything I have commanded you. And surely I will be with you always, to the very end of the age" (Matt. 28:18-20). The disciples were given these instructions to pass onto other disciples so that in every generation, every person in the world would have an opportunity to accept Christ, become a disciple, and be baptized into His kingdom.

If you were asked by another person, "How do I become a Christian? Will you teach me what the Bible says? Help me teach others how to follow Christ," would you be at a loss as to what to say? Most likely our answer would be, "Accept Christ, have faith, go to church, and do the best you can." Most of us really do not know how to start a conversation with a stranger or a friend about spiritual things. If the truth be known, most of us are scared to death to take that risk.

Unfortunately, this demonstrates a lack of faith which silences us and hampers further growth in our relationship with Christ. Many of us do not even know where to find the Scripture passages that validate our faith. These things, which come with a growing spiritual maturity, are important not only for us as men, but for our sons. We set a spiritual example for them which they may well grow up to follow.

Satan cannot defeat us if we continue to talk about Jesus Christ, but he can if we remain silent. Jesus promises to give us the words to say if we will merely open our mouths and place ourselves in those "faith-testing" situations. I have actually taken my sons with me as I walked around the neighborhood meeting neighbors and asking friends to a local home Bible study we attend. This teaches my sons that God is important in my life as I talk about the things I value.

The legacy that we give our sons by our spiritual examples enables us to carry out the Great Commission that Jesus left with us. The promise to be with us "always to the very end of the age" (Matt. 28:20) is one of the best lessons we can teach our sons. We are never alone because Jesus is always beside us. This is a truth that every male, young and old, needs to hold on to if he is to grow spiritually and develop a passion for Christ.

Words to Fathers:

If you're married, ask your wife to answer the questions under the section entitled, "Do I Lead with a Servant Attitude?" according to how she views you as a father. Write down the resolutions for changes you would like to make.

Review the questions about sharing your faith with others from the subsection "Do I Have a Maturing Faith in Christ?" Are you willing to talk with one person today about Jesus? Are you unsure how to begin? Start by letting someone know you have been reading a book on fathers and sons. Discuss this chapter with him and how you feel a need to be more spiritually attuned. Ask him if he ever thinks about the daily role Jesus plays in our lives in introducing us to various situations which could have spiritual solutions. If he shows an interest, find out if he would like to get together and read or study the Bible further.

You will find this can be a very rewarding, natural experience if you are willing to take the chance. However, you will have to become familiar with the Scriptures to lead others. If possible, involve your son in this process by asking him to pray for your witnessing work.

Suggestions for Sons:
Ask your dad if he would be willing to get together on a regular basis so you could both read the Bible together. This allows fathers and sons to grow closer by sharing observations, asking questions, and talking about what verses and stories mean to them and how they apply to their own spiritual needs.

Our conscience testifies that we have conducted ourselves in the world, and especially in our relations with you, in the holiness and sincerity that are from God.

(2 Cor. 1:12)

The reason I came to counseling is because of the way I treat my girlfriend. Whenever we have a disagreement, I become angry, blow up, curse, and break things. My dad used to get angry easily at my mom too. He really had a short fuse. It scared me.

—twenty-one-year-old son

NINE

Teaching Your Son to Be a Lover

IF YOU WERE GOING to teach your son about the ideal man, would you know where to begin? If we took an opinion poll men might tell you that he should be brave, courageous, athletic, and aggressive. Women, on the other hand, might describe him as being strong, gentle, sensitive, dependable, romantic, spiritually-minded, hard-working, and fair.

A 1989 *Psychology Today* survey received 4,500 completed questionnaires from participants answering what they perceived the ideal man to be like. The number one quality of an ideal man, according to this sample of both men and women, was receptiveness and responsiveness to the initiations of others. In other words, most people felt that it was extremely important for a man to listen to what others said to him and to respond in some way that validated the other person. The number one quality basically reflects the Golden Rule (see Matt. 7:12).

Other characteristics in descending order included having a strong intellectual, moral, and physical presence;

paying attention to diet, exercise, and health; expressing feelings of sadness; taking time to wonder, appreciate, and dream; following one's inner authority; being even tempered and moderate; being easy to spend time with; non-judgmentalness; willingness to accept help; and being a "doer" who takes charge. Over 90 percent of the respondents agreed that the ideal man actively cultivated emotional intimacy in friendships. Jesus Christ was ranked first, above all other nominees, as the all-time ideal man, receiving 31 percent of the total vote. The qualities they liked most about Jesus were His caring, loving nature; intelligence; moral honesty; sensitivity; and leadership and courage.[1]

HARSHNESS HARMS BUT PATIENCE PAYS

If you want to know how to have a good relationship, hang around people who have one. One of the most important gifts we can give people is our patience. Patience imparts acceptance. It implicitly reminds them that they are valuable in spite of their mistakes. "Love is patient. It is not rude" (1 Cor. 13:4-5).

One of the leading problems married men succumb to is harshness or impatience toward their wives. This kind of treatment not only undermines a wife's respect for her husband, but it subtly teaches a son that it is all right to verbally mistreat your closest relationships. Some men have been indirectly taught by their fathers' example to use a type of intimidation to gain control of a relationship. Men often use their anger to accomplish this. But frequent and excessive alienating expressions of anger often are a tool by which men hide from their own feelings. In other words, if a man does not discover what feelings are related to his angry reactions, he may never realize what his deepest needs are.

"Calmness can lay great errors to rest" (Ecc. 10:4). Fathers who can maintain patience in the midst of chaos teach their sons how to solve problems instead of escalate them. Crises are a normal part of life and can be remedied one step at a time. Husbands who realize that others need to first feel *understood* before they can *listen* to a different perspective, elicit a great deal of respect from their wives. They also become very proficient problem solvers and peacemakers.

Impatience was probably my greatest weakness in the early years of our marriage. My short fuse and disapproving comments did more to undermine my wife's security than any other behavior. Fortunately, after sixteen years of marriage it only occasionally resurfaces. Regrettably, I now see the same characteristic of impatience in the disposition of one of my sons. I have already begun some preventive maintenance with him. We have had a number of conversations about how much damage impatience can cause in relationships.

Impatience is sometimes exacerbated by fatigue, working too much, or not taking time out to relax and have fun. We all need to unwind daily, maintain our sense of humor, and enjoy one another.

BEING PLAYFUL, SHOWING AFFECTION, AND HAVING FUN

Children love to see their parents having fun together. A son who observes his mother and father enjoying one another's company will imitate that in his future marital relationship. Cultivating a sense of humor enables us to not take ourselves too seriously. Men are very susceptible to becoming entangled in compulsive "busyness" and losing their fun-loving nature. Our sons enjoy seeing their parents kid around, sit and talk together, play tennis, or show affection. In fact, they often love to get in on the action.

When they were younger, my sons used to love to play a

game where I got down on my hands and knees and acted like a monster going after their mother. They would rescue and protect their mother by jumping on me. They loved playing this game because it made them feel like they were saving their mom, and indirectly, though unintentionally, it taught them the importance of being a protector. As they have grown older the poor old monster has been less able to handle their attacks, but we all have fond memories of that time. Now we very much enjoy going on ski trips together as a family, playing tennis, or watching a video at home.

Our sons enjoy seeing Dru-Ann and I go out on dates too. They do not feel left out and are happy that we have an opportunity to go out as a couple. They love to see us expressing affection to each other. I believe this is having a profound effect on them as they already treat females with sensitivity, gentleness, and respect. Recently, Christopher woke up on the wrong side of the bed, and was complaining to his mother about what she had fixed for breakfast. Within a matter of seconds he caught himself, turned around, put his arms around her, and apologized for being mean. He made a genuine effort to be grateful for what she had prepared. It was extremely encouraging to see how he is incorporating respect toward his mother and taking responsibility for himself.

THE DISEASE OF EMOTIONAL DISTANCE AND PREOCCUPATION

Most men do not realize how distant and preoccupied they can be until their wives tell them about it. I commonly hear husbands say to their wives, "Oh, I'm perfectly happy with our relationship," while their wives are feeling, "I'm very unhappy with it." Why this incongruity? The last several generations of fathers have modeled both preoccupation with their work and an emotional unavailability at home. This pattern has not been intentional and most fathers do not plan to be emotionally inaccessible to their families. However, men's relationships with women, their children, work, and themselves have all become ambiguous. Changes in sexual values, the emphasis on materialism, the rise of feminism, and the lack of man-to-man intimacy have become major sources of confusion for men.

Men sometimes feel like they're dancing as fast as they can, and it is still not enough. It causes them to be out of touch with themselves, and therefore with their sons. Men operate under the philosophy: "I'll figure it out myself," "I can handle it," "It doesn't bother me," or "What, me have needs?" This has evidenced itself most destructively in two areas. Men are afraid to emotionally commit themselves to a relationship, and they do not wish to be held accountable for emotional intimacy. They view personal commitment as being trapped in a position where they feel too vulnerable and therefore inadequate. This may seem selfish but at least it is safe. The irony is that these same men will often freely accept accountability within their job and even readily accept more responsibility. This double standard leaves women feeling frustrated. It also models for their sons a fear of intimacy and a confusion over priorities.

Recently a woman in my office while speaking of her relationship with her husband said, "Women take care of men and men take care of themselves." Why are men afraid to be vulnerable and expose their feelings? Perhaps, their feelings of inferiority are nearer the surface than they would like to admit. So to avoid this exposure, men resist becoming involved with anyone. Even when they are living with someone, they often feel alone. They are hesitant to share feelings or thoughts for fear that they might seem inadequate or deficient. They find themselves so busy in work or other activities that they have little time left for true emotional intimacy. They miss out on what true closeness really means because of their preoccupations, self-protectiveness, and suspicious view of others.

Our sons are affected by this in very insidious ways. They feel ignored and sometimes even abandoned because Dad is trying to prove himself and Mom is too busy trying to take care of the rest. As their parents pursue more activities outside of the home, sons are left to fend for themselves. When men abandon family commitment, interpersonal relationships, and responsibility for others and instead pursue acquisition, power, and competition, their sons are sentenced to a life of doing the same.[2]

What can we do about this? Men have to reflect upon their priorities and consider the outcome if they continue in their current direction. Do men really want to be alone? Do they really want to burn out and die at a younger age? As men we must learn to open up, express our feelings, admit our shortcomings, allow ourselves to be vulnerable, and recognize our fear of commitment. We must see other men not simply as competitors but as potential friends. We must listen and change when we hear family and friends tell us, "You're working too much" or "You don't seem to listen."

Relationships need the same kind of time and attention as we commonly give to work. Men need to set time aside for their relationships with their wives and their children. Sons need to see their fathers make their friendships and relationships a priority. A balanced life is necessary to achieve happiness. Men must model for their sons patience, warmth, listening, concern, involvement, and commitment. If fathers can allow themselves to depend on their wives without feeling threatened, and can accept themselves as they are with both their strengths and weaknesses, they can begin relating more comfortably, openly, trustingly, and joyfully.

MODELING EMOTIONAL AND SPIRITUAL INTIMACY

Fathers most clearly model emotional intimacy to their sons in their treatment of their wives. Sons observe years of interactions, patterns, and attitudes between their parents. Their future marital relationships are greatly influenced by their parents' marriages. There are many contexts and levels of intimacy through which fathers can teach their sons to relate to others.[3]

Social intimacy is the most common way that our sons see us interact with others and learn to befriend their peers. It is never too early to begin getting them involved with children their own age. Activities which allow opportunities for social interaction include:

- going to parties,
- talking on the telephone,
- attending movies,
- going out to dinner,
- sharing likes and dislikes,
- relating to others on a casual basis,
- and participating in church youth groups.

Giving your son an opportunity to have friends over for the evening or to accompany the family on outings allows him to gain experience in being with others. Parents also then are able to observe their sons' interactions with others. Teaching them sensitivity to other people's feelings and recognition of their needs are areas where fathers can help their sons learn. Noticing whether or not your son makes good eye contact, speaks to his friends when he sees them, shows warmth and respect, and grows to genuinely like other people, often does not come naturally. He may need input from a concerned, helpful parent. By observing his interactions with others, a father can provide valuable and timely input that may help him in many of his friendships.

Emotional intimacy has to do with sharing feelings on a personal level. The experience of trusting in a friend helps our sons learn to take emotional risks and be vulnerable in relationships. If our sons see us opening up and sharing on a personal level with our wives, they will eventually realize the special bond that husbands and wives can have when they communicate honestly. When occasional difficulties do arise, sons see biblical models of resolution between parents who can talk things out, look for a mutual compromise, apologize where appropriate, and affectionately resolve differences.

Intellectual intimacy occurs as a son grows older. After about seven years old, he becomes fascinated with a number of issues. He may wonder why the sky is different colors at different times, what makes something work, why you cannot see germs, and the rationale behind certain rules. He may begin reading books and finding out interesting facts about animals, airplanes, science, and nature. You will know you are in trouble when one day he asks you, "Why do cars park on driveways and drive on parkways?" or "If airplanes are so safe, why do they call airports terminals?"

The day you realize that your son is a very interesting young man, you will be well on your way to valuing him for the individual he is becoming and admiring him for the unique person he is. When fathers have a genuine interest in learning new things, reading books, and being open to new experiences, they teach their sons that life is fun and readily available to those who pursue it. Husbands and wives who have stimulating discussions regularly also encourage their children to wonder about life and ask questions about what they do not understand.

Spiritual intimacy is the most important area for character building in young children. It enables them to develop an important dimension in their lives that is often ignored or postponed until they can make their own choices.

Fathers are often more comfortable encouraging a son's athletic abilities than their son's spiritual needs. Going to church can be the beginning of this, however, sons will watch their fathers closely to see how authentic their spiritual lives are and emulate that example accordingly. Sometimes wanting children to have a meaningful spiritual influence causes fathers to explore and examine their own beliefs.

There are several spiritual disciplines through which fathers can teach their sons. Praying together bonds a father and a son in a special way. It allows a son to see his dad relate to his Heavenly Father and models an attitude of spiritual intensity, conviction, and respect. It is great for a son to see that his dad has to ask for help too! Sons are encouraged and relieved to see that grown men struggle too and that we all need God to guide us. Rote prayers before meals and at bedtime will not be very helpful here. It is more relevant to have a real conversation with God in the presence of our sons.

Reading the Bible together provides an opportunity to look at how people from years ago developed their own relationships with God. For example, sharing stories about David's struggles as a boy, man, and king complete with his victories and failures, help make the Bible a practical teaching tool for life's experiences. The Book of Proverbs is full of brief bits of wisdom that are just as relevant to our lives today as they were centuries ago. The good news is that the Bible talks about real, not perfect people and their pursuits of a relationship with God.

PROMOTING HEALTHY SEXUAL ATTITUDES

Sexual intimacy is one of the most misunderstood areas a young man faces. However, if a son learns from his father that intimacy involves social, emotional, intellectual, and spiritual dimensions as well, he will have a more healthy, balanced view of sexual intimacy. When the word intimacy is mentioned in our society people immediately think of sex. However, sex is just a small part of learning how to become intimate with another person. Our society has taught us that it is a shortcut to getting to know the opposite sex.

Boys are taught from a young age that having a sexual focus is healthy and favorable. At an early age they are encouraged to be aggressive and to seek fulfillment of their sexual needs whenever the opportunity presents itself. There is no greater way to erode the other dimensions of intimacy than to allow this to occur with your son. Fathers not only have a tremendous responsibility but a great opportunity to shape the sexual attitudes of their sons from an early age.

Fathers, talk to your sons about sexual issues whenever they arise! It is a mistake to avoid all mention of sex because curiosity will lead them to investigate on their own. Share with them the facts of life, appropriate to their age-level, when they are inquisitive about them. Each child is different in terms of what he is capable of understanding. Our sons began asking questions as early as five years old. While not explaining everything, we did supply answers to the questions they had. We continue to clarify and deepen their understanding as different situations arise.

Nowadays it is helpful to discuss television shows or movies when sexual innuendos or suggestive scenes occur. By asking our sons how they felt about certain situations, we can find out their level of understanding and use that as an opportunity to communicate our values with them. The media typically portrays casual sexual involvement with anyone as normal and carrying no consequence. It is important to help our sons have foresight into these situations by helping them see the tragedies that can occur with irresponsible and impulsive behavior.

If parents want their sons to be moral and pure, they must give them good reasons for refraining from sex until they are married. While we may know and respect that this is what God wants us to do, we need to be able to explain the reasons behind our beliefs. We need to help them realize that God recognizes the sexual relationship between a husband and wife as unique and holy. The positive aspects of a sexual relationship with one's wife to be is very important to emphasize. While warning our sons of the potential consequences of sexually immoral behavior alone rarely inhibits them from experimenting, if presented with the healthy aspects mentioned above, it can encourage them to develop true emotional intimacy within their relationships.

Fathers can help sons realize that there will be guilt over going against their own values. There are also risks of pregnancy or acquiring sexually transmitted diseases. Talk to them frequently. It is helpful for them to realize that sexually explicit movies and magazines, or actual experimentation causes one to compare one's future spouse to former lovers. This can undermine one's future marital relationship. It is one of life's great pleasures to be able to share one's first sexual experience with one's mate for life.

Further, a father must be a good model of his own sexual values in his marriage. He must not make sexually provocative jokes, read pornography, watch sexually explicit movies, or stare at other women. Fathers do not realize, but can be assured, that if they have problems with sexual impurity, lust, or infidelity, that their sons will be likewise affected. In my office, it is amazing how many times I find that adult sons ultimately have the same kinds of sexual weaknesses as their fathers did. As men we have a tremendous responsibility and opportunity to shape the attitudes of our sons so that they can have healthy sexual attitudes and experiences in their lives.

REMEMBERING AND CELEBRATING
SPECIAL OCCASIONS

Special occasions offer one of the greatest opportunities fathers have for teaching their sons how to treat women. Many husbands wait until the last minute to plan or find a gift for their wives—giving very little thought or effort. The great advantage of special occasions is that we can plan for them far in advance because the dates are set from the beginning of the year and there are no surprises.

There are absolutely no excuses for a husband to miss a birthday, Christmas, Mother's Day, anniversary, or Valentine's occasion.

Fathers can teach their sons to be thoughtful and plan in advance. This requires a certain sensitivity to the needs of a woman. For instance, a man who knows what his wife would like has a distinct advantage over the husband who does not have a clue. Listing and taking special note of a wife's wishes are in order here. Again, this means planning ahead. Sometimes, why not take your son along and pick out the gift together?

When we include our sons in this planning process, they learn to start ahead of time. They also experience thinking of others before themselves. The excitement of doing something for Mother and seeing Father take a special interest in his wife sets a tremendously healthy precedent for a son's future relationships. He will learn the difference between just giving a present because the calendar dictates it and giving one that is truly from the heart. The private talks, the opportunity to shop together, and the presentation of the gift are all experiences that bond a father and son together and make a wife and mother feel important.

Fathers teach their sons a great deal about how to treat women. Their patience with their wives and family members will leave a lasting impression on their sons which will be carried on into the next generation. Fathers who can be playful, affectionate, and fun-loving will encourage their sons to maintain a similar sense of humor and attitude toward life. By overcoming emotional distance and preoccupations we can tune in to the needs of our family and show our sons the importance of a father who is involved. Dads who can show social, intellectual, emotional, and spiritual intimacy within the family are better equipped to teach healthy sexual attitudes to their sons. When special occasions are remembered and celebrated, both partners in the marriage benefit by deepening their appreciation for each other. Fathers who are wise enough to show their sons this example have given them the most excellent legacy a marriage can receive.

Words to Fathers:
Invite your son to help you plan a special occasion or surprise for his mother. This could be for a birthday or "just because." Take time with him to discuss what she would enjoy, where she might like to go, and how to coordinate the schedule so it will be unexpected. Find an appropriate card for her and go together to look at various choices for a gift. This experience will not only please your wife, but it will teach your son the fun of making this kind of effort for someone you love and appreciate.

Suggestions for Sons:
Ask your dad and mom what their dating experience together was like. What attracted them to each other? How did they meet? How did he treat her? What did she like about him? What made her feel important to him? Get an idea of what makes a woman feel loved, appreciated, and cared for.

Fathers, do not exasperate your children; instead, bring them up in the training and instruction of the Lord.

(Eph. 6:4)

Dear Jim,

As for your concerns about Dad, that's a big issue and I'm not sure I know where to start. I can tell you that I have spent a long time in therapy dealing with it and am just now getting to some closure on it all. It has affected me a great deal, I know that for sure. . . . Dad is not going to change. I have had a hard time accepting that, and have spent my life setting myself up to receive some little acknowledgment or blessing from him only to be disappointed each time. Somewhere along the way I stopped trying. I will always miss him, though. There will always be a hollow place inside of me where love and acceptance from him should have been. That is something I can never change. . . . There is something he is afraid of: sharing, communicating, allowing another person to be okay, and respecting differing opinions. Other ways of viewing life threaten him and so he cannot do that. Does he love us? Yes, in his own way. Is that enough for me? No, I need him to know and love me for the person I am.

—one brother to another about their dad

TEN

A Closer Look at Homosexuality: Searching for Daddy?

I HAVE A GREAT DEAL of compassion for anyone who struggles with emotional and physical attraction toward the same sex. Homosexual tendencies often antagonize and alienate an individual from an early age, causing him to feel very different from his peers. You may remember how hard it was being young, trying to understand yourself, fit in with friends, and make sense of what life was supposed to be about. Add to this, confusion over unexplained sexual feelings toward someone of the same sex, and the outcome is a very complicated identity problem.

Homosexuality is a controversial yet delicate subject. There are an estimated 25 million homosexuals and lesbians in the United States alone.[1] We cannot afford to simply write off this segment of our society because we feel their problems will not affect us. Few people understand homosexuality and so it legitimately scares them. In response, the homosexual community labels heterosexuals' fear of gays as homophobia. Touché! It is time we had a little more understanding on both sides.

Almost every homosexual describes a process of evolving into, becoming aware of, or accepting their "gayness." Many struggle with their identity confusion and take years to come to terms with that reality and "come out" publicly. Those who have been practicing homosexuals for years, tend to forget this evolution and maintain they were "always this way." I believe a *continuum of homosexuality* exists in which a person first questions his identity as a male, then struggles with *dystonic* homosexual feelings, and after years of confusion and discomfort becomes an *ego-syntonic* homosexual.

Dystonic homosexuality is where a male has attractions and feelings for other men but wishes he did not. He would prefer to be straight and have heterosexual urges, and he, in fact, may have some. While the homosexual community might prefer to call such persons bisexuals, I believe these individuals are still very confused about their identities and looking for other explanations. Dystonic homosexuals can turn the tide of their sexual development and effectively orient to a heterosexual lifestyle if they want to do so and seek to get treatment.

Egosyntonic homosexuals have already proceeded so far down the continuum of homosexuality that they are often uninterested or unwilling to consider the possibility of a heterosexual reorientation. They are often insulted and infuriated if that option is even suggested. Unfortunately, the current trend in psychological literature suggests that homosexuals have prenatal brain hormonalization which influences one's subsequent sexual status or orientation. Therefore, allegedly nothing can be done to change or influence their sexual fate. The evidence is inconclusive, yet represents the current popular trend of assigning responsibility for the way we are to genes, heredity, physiology, or hormones. This view places little responsibility upon the individual, family, environment, or outside influences which have a significant effect on one's identity. It also ignores the concept of "free choice." The physiological approach predestines one to a sexual orientation, and it leaves no chance to alter that destiny.

My clinical experiences and those of many of my professional peers are different. We have had successes with homosexuals who are unhappy with their lifestyles and want to experience a heterosexual orientation. But the physiologic explanation is too simplistic and deterministic. It underestimates the innate power within each of us to direct his own life. I am ethically unwilling to work with a homosexual who is convinced of his sexual orientation and not open to change.

The dystonic homosexual, on the other hand, is often open to change and sincerely willing to do whatever he can to orient to a heterosexual lifestyle. I would like to focus on those individuals, the causes of their dystonic homosexuality, and the success that has been experienced by many who prefer a way out of this identity epidemic.

PUBLIC POLARITY OVER HOMOSEXUALITY

Homosexuality is a divisive issue in contemporary culture. Heterosexuals, by and large, prefer to ignore homosexual issues in hopes that they will go away. The gay community, on the other hand, would like to see homosexuality accepted and normalized as a legitimate lifestyle. They argue for equal rights and the same representation that heterosexual couples have with marriage licenses, family health insurance, adoption of children, and inclusion of spouses as legal heirs.

Both sides have extremist groups who only seem to aggravate the situation. On the side *against* homosexuals, terms like faggot, queer, pervert, child molester, and deviant are commonly used. Some feel AIDS is God's punishment on the over 50,000 gays that have already died and even hope the disease will eliminate the problem by wiping out the homosexual population.

On the militant side *for* homosexuality, such shock

groups as ACT-UP (AIDS Coalition to Unleash Power) are picketing, breaking up meetings, yelling obscenities at the opposition, engaging in public displays of sexually explicit behavior, and even initiating violence against others. This group feels that if it does not act in extremist ways, supportive AIDS legislation may not be forthcoming.

The truth is that the AIDS epidemic has affected both the homosexual and the heterosexual communities through blood transfusions, heterosexual encounters with HIV positive infected individuals, intravenous drug users, and babies born to mothers who have AIDS. It is not just a homosexual problem any longer. However, gay militant groups such as ACT-UP have used and exploited the AIDS tragedy to promote a wider acceptance of their lifestyle.

Neither of these approaches are adequate; they will only worsen and complicate the complex problems we are facing. Cooperation and understanding are needed by all people. We are all human beings regardless of whether we agree with each other or have a personal relationship with God. He made us and He loves us all.

BOYS NEED MEN

One of the earliest interpersonal psychological theories suggested a dominant mother and absent father combination as a cause of homosexuality. This idea has been refuted, labeled as simplistic, and emphatically criticized as invalid—especially by gays. While it does have its limitations, it is a contributing variable with some merit.

There is no simple explanation for the causal factors involved in homosexuality. However, one area that has received very little in-depth review is the effect of the father-son relationship. In essence, a mother's dominance with her son has been considered the culprit in the past, and the father's lack of involvement or abusive involvement was considered secondary.

The rest of this chapter will review what may be the greatest outside factor in determining a son's sexual orientation—his father's influence. Boys need men to help them learn how to identify with and become comfortable with their masculinity. The depth and quality of a father-son relationship affects a boy more than most ever realize.

The United States is often accused of being patriarchal. There is a lot of evidence to support this, especially in the different pay scales that men and women receive. Men do seem to command more respect than women, and this certainly is unfair in many areas.

In response to women's second class status, the feminist movement began arguing for the equality of men and women. To our benefit, it exposed a patriarchal society that oppressed women. As much as the women's movement has enabled half of our society to experience greater freedom and equality, it has also served to reduce the value of men. This was not the intent of the women's movement, however as a result, men have become uninvolved, neutralized, and tentative in their roles. They have taken a passive position in important matters such as emotions, family, and relationships, focusing more on their jobs, accomplishments, and financial acquisitions. In effect, men have lost their identity. They no longer pull together as men looking for the company of other men. In general, men are quite alone nowadays.

There is some indication that a men's movement is on the horizon, however. There is even a male-oriented treatment program in Houston, Texas where only men are allowed to participate.[2] Many of these men typically have substance abuse or alcohol problems. When men can find affirmation for their feelings within a group of other men, they develop more confidence. Our culture encourages young boys to ignore their inner feelings while teaching young girls to tune into theirs. The experience of this men's group has found that approximately 40 percent of all men have serious regrets about the time and effort that they put into succeeding. They wished they would have exchanged some of their success for spending more time with their wives and children. The program believes that if a man has grown up without a significantly involved father, emotional deficits are likely to have occurred. Their treatment program enables men to experience their feelings and to be involved in that process with other men.

When men talk about the anger they feel toward their fathers, it's amazing how vividly they describe the incidents—even ones that happened as long as thirty years ago. An absent father creates deep feelings of regret and anger. Adult sons feel that their fathers refused to give them what they needed.[3]

Most men never reveal the anger they feel toward their fathers. Sadness is the dominant feeling beneath their anger. Especially when they realize that their father-son relationship may never be close. It is not impossible for such a loss to be reconciled. It is a painful process that does not occur quickly, but it is certainly worth the effort. It is never too late to experience reparation between a father and son. Even if only a small portion of that relationship can be restored or cultivated, it can make a lasting difference.

GOD'S VIEW OF HOMOSEXUALITY

You probably have at least one personal problem that no matter how well under control, if left unattended, will return to hamper you again. This problem may have begun at an early age and still plagues you into adulthood. Even the Apostle Paul noted a "thorn in my flesh" that he asked God on a number of occasions to remove (2 Cor. 12:7). Homosexuality is that problem for some people. It comes complete with so many other related problems that it is often overwhelming. It is made even more difficult to deal with by the severe identity problems with which most homosexuals struggle.

Further, they have incomplete character formations and deficits which make it hard to find and maintain specific codes of ethics in their lives. But it is reasonable to expect that homosexuals can change, even though they may continue to deal with their urges for years to come.

Homosexuality has existed from the beginning of time. Early in the Old Testament the men from Sodom approached Lot's house and wanted to have sex with the two angels. The angels in response blinded all of the homosexuals and later destroyed the city (Gen. 19:1-10).

Old Testament law also offers specific prohibitions against homosexuality. Leviticus 18:22 states, "Do not lie with a man as one lies with a woman; that is detestable." While Leviticus 20:13 tells us, "If a man lies with a man as one lies with a woman, both of them has done what is detestable."

Throughout the New Testament homosexuality is addressed not merely as an alternate lifestyle, but as a behavior that is wrong in God's eyes. Actually, God sees any kind of immorality as wrong. Paul writes:

> *It is God's will that you should be holy; that you should avoid sexual immorality; that each of you should learn to control his own body in a way that is holy and honorable, not in passionate lust like the heathen, who do not know God; and that in this matter no one should wrong his brother or take advantage of him. The Lord will punish men for all sorts of sins, as we have already told you and warned you. For God did not call us to be impure, but to live a holy life. Therefore, he who rejects this instruction does not reject man, but God who gives you His Holy Spirit (1 Thes. 4:3-8).*

God considers homosexuality a perversion of His intentions. Romans 1:18-32 describes God's wrath against humanity. Scripture says that "the wrath of God is being revealed from heaven against all the godlessness and wickedness of men who suppress the truth" (v. 18). It further proclaims that "God gave them over to sinful lusts. Even their women exchanged natural relations for unnatural ones. In the same way the men also abandoned natural relations with women and were inflamed with lust for one another" (vv. 26-27). Homosexuality is seen as a natural consequence of rebellion against God. Ultimately, homosexuals will not inherit the kingdom of God (1 Cor. 6:9-10).

As strong as Scripture is in condemning homosexual practice, God still loves homosexuals as people. All of us are His children and He wants us to remain close to Him. When that relationship is severed, it is because we have chosen to go our own way and disregard His will for our lives. Jesus reminded us that His words would be our judge on the last day. The words He left for us to live by will judge all of us who do not follow them. We do have a choice to accept or reject the words Jesus left for us from His Father. But remember, they will be the standard by which each of us will be measured (John 12:47-50).

THE FATHER-SON RELATIONSHIP: A PRIMARY INFLUENCE

In 1962 Irving Bieber wrote *Homosexuality: A Psychoanalytic Study of Male Homosexuals*. In his book he described family dynamics which fostered a son's homosexual identity. These dynamics included an overprotective mother and an absent father. In such a relationship the mother favored the son over the father, demanded the son's attention, and even could be seductive toward him. According to psychoanalytic theory, the mother discouraged masculine activities in favor of more feminine behaviors. Mom made her son her closest confidant and actually pitted him against her husband. The theory suggests that the father was often hostile toward his son for coming between him and his wife while the mother displaced her affection, which should have been directed toward her husband, onto her son. The son naturally felt rejected by his father and was often afraid of him. The father was seen as distant and hostile, and little or no relationship existed between them. Naturally the marital relationship was poor, and perhaps originally the core problem.

Since Bieber's landmark study there has been a great deal of public outcry from the homosexual community disputing his theories. Dr. Charles Silverstein, author of *Man to Man: Gay Couples in America,* holds that the psychoanalytic theory of the distant father and overprotective mother is merely a myth.

In all fairness, the worst that can be said about the psychoanalytic viewpoint is that it only examines one of the many family interactional variables that contribute to the identity formation of homosexuality. Other possible family interactional variables include: a dominant, critical father and a weak, ineffectual mother; two emotionally uninvolved parents; a rejecting mother and a weak father; an emotionally over-involved mother who is sexually indiscreet and makes her son her peer and confidant, especially in the absence of a father; or two rejecting parents with substance abuse problems. Still other influential factors can include poor role models; learned feminine overidentification; feelings of rejection from males; mild genetically inherited or hormonally induced effeminate characteristics; emotional or sexual abuse, or premature sexual stimulation in early years; unresolved fear and confusion about the same or opposite sex; feelings of inadequacy, low self-esteem, social awkwardness; and rejection of one or both parents by the child.

WHAT THE RESEARCH SHOWS

The research into the causes of and influences upon homosexuality is controversial, confusing, and generally inconclusive. There are some consistent trends, however, that bear noting and warrant further inquiry.

Tim LaHaye has noted that he had never counseled a homosexual who had a good relationship with his father. While he considers the father as only the secondary influence in the son's life, it is my position that the father plays the primary influence role in the identification process of homosexuals.[4]

Joseph Nicolosi, a psychologist who works at the Thomas Aquinas Psychological Clinic in Encino, California, practices reparative therapy with homosexuals. He supports the view that homosexual feelings in males are a psychological condition that are a result of "incomplete masculine identification." Nicolosi postulates that homosexuality is a result of a man's rejection by other men beginning with his father. In his practice, he has noted that all his clients have had poor relationships with their fathers.[5]

Richard Green, M.D., is professor of Psychiatry at the UCLA School of Medicine, and author of *The Sissy Boy Syndrome and the Development of Homosexuality*. He followed forty-four feminine boys from early childhood to adulthood. In this longitudinal study he discovered patterns in parents who encouraged feminine type behaviors while discouraging masculine behaviors. They denied their sons' male identities and actually contributed to their feelings of inadequacy and low self-esteem by pushing them toward a feminine identity which can contribute to a homosexual orientation. Green also noted patterns of fathers who rejected their feminine sons. Green noted that fathers are the most important influence on their sons' development into men. He recommended that fathers remain close to their sons by modeling the virtues they want them to emulate.[6]

In a twelve year project conducted by psychologists Alan Bell, Martin Weinberg, and Sue Kiefer Hammersmith of the Kinsey Institute for Research in Sex, Gender, and Reproduction, the lives and backgrounds of over 1,300 men and women were surveyed. The participants were racially mixed as well as homosexual and heterosexual. Of all the subjects in this sample, homosexual men reported less positive relationships with their fathers than did heterosexual men.[7]

Elizabeth Moberly, a research psychologist in Cambridge, England, maintains that most men who engage in homosexual behavior do so because of the deficit in the relationship with their fathers. The drive for homosexuality is fueled by wanting to fill this deficit.[8]

Another psychologist, Bobby Reed, also believes that an early negative experience with a father is a contributing factor which could influence a son's homosexual orientation. She maintains that all boys need healthy, positive relationships with fathers or father figures to help develop their masculine identity. Furthermore, she recommends finding role models by requesting assignments to classes taught by men in the public school or at church, hiring male sitters, and involving sons in Boy Scouts, Little League, or Big Brother organizations.[9]

The experience of these clinicians and researchers consistently points to problems in the father-son relationship where homosexuality has become the son's orientation. In addition, it is important to note that rejection occurs on both sides. That is to say, the father may reject his son by not approving of him or ignoring him. However, the son likewise rejects his father by refusing to identify with or model after him.

Men in our society are discouraged from being closely involved with other men. They may admire others from afar, but it is rarely verbalized and often demonstrated by intense competition between men. This relegates men to lonely lifestyles of acquiring, producing, and proving one's self to other men. The most many sons get from their fathers is a handshake and a pat on the back for a job well done. Their deepest needs of acceptance, approval, and affection are often ignored because men in our society are not supposed to openly care for other men. This leaves men very vulnerable to an "incomplete masculine identification."

THE BIOLOGICAL ARGUMENT
FOR HOMOSEXUALITY

Over the last decade the causes of all types of psychological behavior have been examined from a biological perspective. Research has sought to find a hormonal, genetic, or physiologic factor to explain behavior trends.[10] There are several problems with this biological focus. The most obvious shortcoming is that the research is typically performed on animals and then the results are often generalized toward humans. This is always dangerous since human beings have the most developed intellect of all beings and hardly compare to lower animals.

Secondly, research results have to be statistically significant, and therefore, repeatable in order to draw unrefutable conclusions. Many of the experiments report results as "approaching significance" or "indicating trends somewhat supportive of" this or that hypothesis. Many of these research projects merely generate more questions requiring further research and often obscure or complicate the original question.

Thirdly, biologically-oriented research tends to remove personal responsibility, choice, and outside influence from the individual and attribute human behavior to causes out of an individual's focus of control. Research provides an important contribution to our society in solving some of the difficult problems of our lives, but overgeneralizing results can create additional problems instead of resolving them.

A recent article in the *American Psychological Association Monitor* noted that research may be moving away from the biological explanation of homosexuality.[11] Many of the current ideas are still speculative and methodological flaws exist in the research. However, in the psychological community there is general acceptance that biological factors do influence one's sexual orientation.

Homosexuals have used the biological argument as a platform to validate their lifestyle and to disqualify any attempts to find other causal factors. In actuality, gays do not want any psychological explanation for their lifestyle because it would detract from their attempts to establish homosexuality as innate and inborn. Homosexuals who do not wish to change their lifestyle will probably not be open to any other explanations anyway. Therefore, the focus in counseling should be geared toward those individuals who wish to change their orientation. Currently the American Psychological Association's committee on Lesbian and Gay Concerns is considering a resolution that would recommend that attempts to change the sexual orientation of a homosexual be considered unethical.[12] This resolution is important because it basically violates the rights of those who legitimately "seek" sexual reorientation, and disallowing them treatment would be grossly unethical and discriminatory.

The biological view argues for the existence of innate influences upon the sexual orientation of human beings. While there is some validity to their claims, there is no evidence to suggest that these differences cannot be overcome, compensated for, or channeled in healthier ways. Physical disabilities, handedness, learning disabilities, physical stature, specific talents, or intellectual abilities represent areas where many have been biologically short-changed. Resigning ourselves to these could be tragic indeed.

It would be a gross error to overemphasize the biological perspective to the exclusion of the many psychological influences we are exposed to throughout our lives. It would also underestimate our tremendous ability to compensate for personal limitations. The average layperson cannot intelligently argue with the biological explanations given because he or she is not a scientist. However, clinically there are many cases of individuals who, by the biological definition, should be homosexual but are not. There are still others who have homosexual urges, but who prefer heterosexuality. A person who chooses the homosexual life has a right to refuse other lifestyle alternatives, but he does not have a right to limit others' explorations for change. The danger of the biological argument is that it attempts to predestine homosexuals to that lifestyle with little, if any, hope for other alternatives they might choose.

HELPING TO DEVELOP A MASCULINE IDENTITY

Fathers can help their sons develop a masculine identity by making them feel wanted as important members of the family. When a son feels accepted and loved he is more apt to feel close to others. Separation, rejection, and alienation from one's father are major contributors to the "incomplete masculine identification" syndrome. Fathers, try the following:

- acknowledge your son's role in the family,
- greet him in the morning,
- make eye contact with him when speaking,
- smile and say "I love you" daily,
- praise him when he tries to accomplish something.

There are still other conscious disciplines we can practice to encourage masculinity. Take a look at the following examples to see which ones you need to incorporate into your relationships.

(1) *Be patient and gentle with your son, reassuring him that mistakes are a natural part of life.* Develop an atmosphere that is predictable. Many sons describe their father's temper and moods as unpredictable and so avoid much needed contact with their dad. Be approachable and receptive so that your son can feel safe in bringing his problems to you.

(2) *Let him know when you see characteristics of yourself in him.* Do this when you see gestures, talents, or interests that remind you of your childhood. This helps him to relate to you as a man. Share shortcomings or struggles you had growing up and how you overcame or compensated for those difficulties. It will help him feel like his problems are not unique. This helps sons to identify with fathers and not be so hard on themselves.

(3) *Help your son face his fears, insecurities, and reluctance to try new things by doing them with him.* Praise every effort. Encourage him to get other friends to try new experiences together with him. Make a game out of it. Do not criticize him, put him down, or give up on him. His effort is what counts. Even if he is not as naturally talented as you were, helping him develop motivation through your praise will help him compensate.

(4) *Do things regularly with him man-to-man.* Take him to breakfast, jog together, go bowling, play catch, kick the soccer ball, watch a movie, get ice cream together, read a book, go fishing, wrestle with him, or play video games. Choose an activity that you can both enjoy together.

(5) *Freely show him affection.* Boys need daily hugs, touching, rough-housing, and physical contact with their dads. Affection fills an inner need that words cannot. If affection is uncomfortable to you, solicit some help by talking with others, getting some counseling, cultivating closer male friends, or joining a men's group to work on your personal issues.

(6) *Help him become interested in some activity, sport, or talent that he can feel proficient in.* Nothing builds confidence more than knowing that you are good at something. Many times kids who struggle with self-esteem problems compensate by showing strengths in at least one other area.

(7) *Talk about and encourage male and female friendships.* If your son does not have boys his own age in the neighborhood, invite them home with him from school, church, or Scouts. Let him know it is all right to be interested in girls

too. As a man, demonstrate acceptance of women by treating your own wife with respect, patience, equality, and affection. Do not tease your son about his curiosity with girls, but reinforce his interest. Help him to talk about it.

(8) *Teach him social skills to help him compensate if he is shy, awkward, or introverted.* Help him to properly use the phone, join a group, start a conversation, handle an argument, or treat others in a warm and friendly manner.

(9) *Encourage him to freely express his emotions and feelings.* If your son grows up internalizing his feelings and not expressing what he thinks, his silence will eventually isolate him from you. An attitude of openness will foster avenues of closeness and acceptance in your relationship with him.

(10) *Encourage your son to develop discipline, responsibility, and dependability.* Help him to finish what he starts by doing it together with him, if necessary. Advocate that he stick with his commitments and do his part. Assign him things within the home that he can do and be responsible for regularly. Help him learn to never give up and to persevere through school, projects, chores, and difficult situations. This builds character and helps him to feel good about his accomplishments. It also combats impulsiveness and defeat. This may take a lot of your time initially, but it will save you grief and frustration in the long run.

(11) *Model a positive, healthy, affectionate relationship with your wife.* This bears repeating. It helps a son relish closeness, unity, and harmony. It teaches cooperation and teamwork as a couple and family. Show mutual nonsexual affection freely and openly. Such modeling will affect his relationships with women the rest of his life.

(12) *Finally, fathers need to have close male friends so that their sons can see them interacting with other men.* Men who demonstrate such friendships also help sons to learn to relate to other males. Men who are loners, quiet, withdrawn, or friendless teach their sons by default that friend-

ships with other men are not important. Too much inwardness fosters isolation, living through fantasies, and self-centeredness.

Various kinds of involvement in relationships helps a son to enjoy being male. It develops his identification with both boys and men and encourages him to experience healthy and well-rounded relationships with both men and women. Fathers play a big role in positively shaping the attitudes of their sons. Even if your son is more effeminate than you are comfortable with, he can still compensate if you show patience, encouragement, and acceptance. Our sons need to feel we love them no matter what.

WHAT IF I DISCOVER MY SON IS GAY?

If you suspect or know that your son has been involved in homosexual activity, do not panic. Above all, do not withdraw from or reject him. Try to realize that this is an identity problem that has tormented *him* much more than it has alarmed *you*. Try to work through your initial shock if you need to, and then find some opportunities to sit down and discuss this with him. Let love, patience, and understanding be your guide.

Do not ridicule, criticize, or degrade your son for his orientation. I have seen many occasions where a renewed father-son relationship began the process of reconciliation and the son's feelings of homosexuality subsided. It is never too late to cultivate a relationship with your son. There may be a number of barriers to overcome and prejudices to work through, but my experience is that boys or men want their father's love and acceptance no matter how long they have lived without it.

If your son is receptive to counseling, find a counselor or psychologist who is familiar with homosexuality. (A list of organizations providing healing for the homosexual is located in the appendix.) There are a number of mental health professionals whose familiarity simply consists of encouraging the acceptance of one's sexual orientation. If your son is not interested in examining or evaluating his sexual orientation then you may have to be patient and continue building your relationship. Trying to force him into treatment when he is uninterested in changing will insure inevitable failure.

In working with homosexuals, my experience is that they can make a shift in sexual orientation if they are interested and motivated in thoroughly examining the possibilities. If they are simply making a change for their parents or someone else, it is rarely effective. Changing their sexual orientation will be perhaps the hardest thing they ever try to do. Treatment takes approximately one year at the minimum and often involves family counseling.

If you're faced with such a crisis, continue loving your son and deepening your relationship with him. Accepting him does not mean accepting his lifestyle. Eventually, the closeness that you develop may make a difference in his future.

Words to Fathers:
If your young son demonstrates characteristics that you feel are effeminate and unappealing, consider the following. All sons need and want to identify with another male—preferably you. Even cautious, awkward, or soft kids can learn to compensate with the involvement of a concerned man.

Remember, what you focus upon you strengthen! If you constantly criticize certain negative traits, you will inadvertently reinforce these. Praise him at every opportunity. Be involved in activities he likes to do and he will excel in them. Compensating in areas of talents helps a son feel he is good at something. This will generalize to his trying new and different tasks. Your involvement will cause him to gravitate toward other males for friendship and camaraderie. He will want to do what the other boys are doing because of a desire to identify with them.

This model of wanting to identify with the same sex begins with a positive, accepting, and involved relationship with a father or another significant older male. Don't worry if your son is not as rough, athletic, or tough as the other kids his age—he will develop in those areas if you believe in him and accept him for who he is now.

Suggestions for Sons:

If you have struggled with occasional or persistent physical attraction for men or had sexual encounters with them, yet regret those urges or experiences, there is something you can do. Talk to someone. Alcoholics Anonymous has a slogan that says: "You're only as sick as your secrets." When we share our secrets with another person, the power of their effects upon us diminish. You will probably feel this would be too risky—however, you cannot afford to keep it to yourself. It will dominate your thinking, reinforce the urges, and set you up to possibly act out again. At the very least, it will keep you emotionally alienated from others.

I have spoken to dozens of men who wanted to change their behavior but were unwilling to talk about it—especially with a close friend or family member. Those who made progress in overcoming their homosexual tendencies eventually shared their secrets with those closest to them. While some people may not initially handle such a disclosure well, most will offer support, love, and understanding to a loved one who is sincere in his efforts to change.

This is a leap of faith but one that can change the course of a life and allow the opportunity for eternal happiness.

When he came to his senses, he said, " . . . I will set out and go back to my father." . . . But while he was still a long way off, his father saw him and was filled with compassion for him; he ran to his son, threw his arms around him and kissed him.

(Luke 15:17-20)

Dear Son,

As you know, your grandfather has been very ill lately. It has caused me to examine our lives and the status of our relationship. I realize he may not live much longer so I feel an urgency to make amends with him where necessary. Our talks have been very encouraging and enlightening to say the least. We were not that close when I was younger and I have often resented that. I have learned through our talks that he wanted to be closer, but did not know how.

Ironically, this discovery has made me aware of something else. You and I have not been that close either, and now I understand a little better why that is. I am writing to ask if we might try to correct this. I'm not exactly sure what to do about it, but I know I would like to try. It would mean a lot to me.

—fifty-three-year-old father

ELEVEN

The Power of
the Past

HAS THIS BOOK made you aware of some needs or unfinished business you have with your father or son? Maybe you would like to understand that relationship better or compare what you experienced with what others have realized. Hearing about other people's lives or reading personal accounts of their problems usually helps us to under stand our own more clearly. This final chapter includes a variety of letters *to fathers and about fathers* that may stir certain relevant memories or feelings you have had. Read these letters carefully and allow God to speak to you about your father-son relationship past, present, and future.

When you think of your father a number of thoughts, feelings, images, recollections, and regrets probably flood your senses. Perhaps you recall what a good dad he was— so strong, smart, and talented. He may have been a lot of fun and had a terrific sense of humor. Maybe he was ready to play games whenever you asked. Perhaps you remember singing together and making up rhymes. Your father taught you a lot, even if you didn't always agree with him.

Do you remember a father who used to sneak up behind your mom and hug, squeeze, tickle, and kiss her? Those moments may have elicited giggles from the kids, but most children love to see their parents expressing affection.

Perhaps you recall how easily he could talk to the neighbors. If you were lucky, perhaps he had buddies with whom he would do things occasionally, and sometimes even invite you along. If he was affectionate, fair, sensitive, and attentive to your feelings, you were fortunate indeed. Children miss dads like these because such fathers leave behind a legacy of fond memories: a time when their sons experienced a unique relationship with the big fellow they called *Dad*.

Some sons are not so lucky. You may be one of them. You missed having the kind of special relationship described above. Perhaps your dad was rarely present or only able to visit every other weekend because of custody arrangements. Or, did your father live at home but was never available to you? Maybe you remember a father who was always working. You may have a lot of emotional regrets and anger toward a dad who never seemed to have enough time for you. This kind of emotional unavailability made you wonder, "What's wrong with me?" or "I guess I'm not good enough."

Some sons have dads who have never been very nice to them. Did your dad always seem to be in a bad mood when he came home from work? You may feel that you never did anything right—at least according to your dad. Some sons grow up terrified of their fathers because of the harsh treatment, angry words, and violent behavior they experienced.

Whether you grew up having a positive or a negative experience with your father, you look back on those times with a wide array of feelings. Following are a number of letters written by sons to their fathers expressing appreciation, regret, anger, resentment, and thankfulness. Some of these will make you smile, while others may trigger feelings that you have not experienced in a number of years.

LETTERS TO DAD

Here is a letter from my oldest son to me after a fun day at the office together.

Dear Dad,

I'm glad you are my dad! It was fun with you in the office. I had a good time. I hope I get to do it again with you another time.

> *Your son,*
> *Chris*

The next letter is from a talented and capable thirty-year-old man who felt he never could please his father. Struggling to find himself, he was constantly a disappointment to his father and himself.

Dad,

It's been a long time since I've written a letter to you. I found some old letters that you had written me and I hadn't reread them in a long time. As you know I'm in counseling. I've completed three sessions and my next one is today. I feel comfortable about moving forward to know myself better. I'm seeing a Christian counselor and this is very motivating and inspirational to me. Mom told me that you had asked how my sessions were going. I was happy to know that you had inquired. That means a lot to me.

Dad, there are some things that bother me and have been on my mind, but I just don't know how to approach you with them. How do you feel about our relationship as father and son? Dad, I love you and have the highest respect for you. It feels good to tell others of you. I've encountered many men and there is no one who compares in terms of strength, leadership, priorities, punctuality, and more. I'm not just saying that because you're my father. I really mean it.

I don't know if you have noticed it or not, but I take most of my problems to Mom. I know that a lot of my discussions are repetitious and you would be the first to tell me. Whether you know it or not — that hurts. I can pretty much expect the same response from you. I guess that's why I'm hesitant to talk to you about those problems. More than anything I want us to be like friends, but you're my father and maybe that's asking too much of you. I don't know why I'm afraid to talk to you about my problems. Over the years I've taken you through changes and I'm sorry. As a father you have the right to get upset when you feel used, or disappointed in me. However, I wish we could talk more about those things. I guess I'm afraid you might yell at me or hit me if I say something that is out of line.

I can still remember you telling me that, at times, you didn't like me very much. I wish we had the kind of relationship where the two of us could get away and really get to know each other better. Dad, what you think and how you feel means a lot to me. I hesitate to tell you what all is really going on with me because my life is in such a shambles.

I do have a new female friend who "gets on" me when I mess up or dwell on the negative aspects of myself. She is trying to get me to look at my positive strengths. She wants me to say exactly what I feel and not worry about what other people might think. I guess that's why it's been so easy for me to go to Mom in the past, because she would listen, give me feedback, and not put me down. I know that you and Mom handle things differently, and I really can't ask you to change, but I do need your approval.

I know that I have frustrated you in the past when you have tried to help me, but I would like to try again. I hope we can listen to each other's points of view, even if they are different.

Your son,
Jim

The preceding letter is about a son who still very much longs for his father's approval. His father has repeatedly been disappointed with him and has freely expressed that.

In situations like this both father and son have responsibility for repairing a strained relationship. Fathers and sons who remain in this state of emotional separation must begin forgiving each other. Without this forgiveness they can never honestly face their own problems and begin to reconcile their relationship.

Next is a letter from a middle-aged man who is still desperately seeking his father's approval and love. Although he would be considered successful by most people's standards, this son still sees himself as floundering in life without a clear identity.

Dear Dad,

I'm writing this letter because I need your advice and your help. It seems I don't like myself very much and I'm trying to understand why. Maybe I can learn to like myself a bit more or change into someone more likable. I'm trying to understand how I came to be who I am.

I know that to a large degree I am a product of you and maybe by understanding you better, I can understand myself. When I look at you I see many qualities that I admire, but some that I don't like at all. Of all your good qualities, the ones I admire the most are your willingness to work two jobs as we were growing up to provide for us, your dedication to Mom and the family, your skill in building and fixing many things around the house, your patience in doing a job well, your humility and planning vacations for us.

Among the qualities that I don't like are your sensitivity to being hurt when we disagreed with you in any way, the way you ordered Mom around in expecting her to do whatever you wanted, and your frugality with money.

I guess the thing that bothers me most is that I see in me the qualities about you I don't like, but few, if any, of the qualities I do like. Dad, I just want to be a man and be happy with myself. I want your strengths but not your weaknesses. I want to be worthy of someone loving me.

You've said so often that Mom was too good to you. Because of your good points she has learned to accept your faults. Mom is a really good woman and she deserves better treatment from you. I know that you love Mom very much and that she knows it too. But it hurts me when I see how you treat her sometimes.

I also want to be a good man in a relationship, but I don't know how. I feel so insecure and threatened by women. I'm jealous of their friends or their job success, and I feel so stupid sometimes around them.

When I look back, Dad, I wonder what could have been different. You're a good man who loved his family. As a role model, perhaps, you weren't as dynamic as you might have been. But, I remember wanting to be just like you.

This job I'm in right now makes me feel stupid and inadequate. Remember how much I wanted you to be proud of me? You really were when I got hired, but I know I let you down when I dropped out of college to join the Air Force. I'll never know if I did the right thing, but I did what I did.

It does occur to me that many of my decisions seem wrong in retrospect so maybe that one was too. You know, Dad, maybe if I could have seen you love yourself, I might have learned to love myself.

Your son,
Al

The next narrative is not a letter from a son to his father, but a recollection of a son's past memories of his dad. He writes about a number of missed opportunities and regrets that caused him to feel cheated out of the influence his father might have had on him.

It's not that I miss my dad. I don't. I never really knew him so I can't miss him per se. What I do miss are the things we should have shared, the things we should have done together. I watch other dads and their sons. Sometimes it hurts to watch them. I wish I could have done with my dad the things they do with theirs.

I wish I could have spent more time with my dad. I wish we could have gone bowling, fishing, or to a movie together. I wish we could have just sat and talked to each other. I never confided in my dad. We never talked about girls, dating, love, life, sex, or anything. My dad was a businessman at work and at home. He never had time for me.

I don't blame my dad. I know he had a lot of the same problems I do. His relationship with his dad was like mine and my dad.

I never saw my dad being intimate with my mom. I never learned how to be intimate. It's still hard for me. I don't know how to deal with it. It makes me uncomfortable.

I only saw my dad angry once. He lost control and beat me. There were welts on my legs. My mom and sister had to pull him off me. He never got angry again. I rarely lose my temper. When I do I explode. I saw my dad cry only once when he caught me smoking. I was so ashamed. I still smoke, but I almost never cry in front of people.

My dad never held me. He never touched me. He never told me he loved me or was proud of me. I know he did love me and I know he was proud of me, but he couldn't tell me.

I never argued with my dad. I never asked his opinion or his advice. He had zero influence on my life and life decisions, or so I thought. Now I have discovered I am just like my dad.

It's too late to change things between my dad and myself. He died eleven years ago. I wish I could tell him I'm sorry and I love him. If nothing else, he was my dad.

> *Regretfully,*
> *Richard*

The following is an excerpt from an adult son in his thirties who came to counseling because he never felt accepted by his male friends. He was struggling with his own sense of identity and what path he should take vocationally at that point in his life. His uninvolved, emotionally abusive father left him a legacy of poor self-esteem.

As a teenager my dad's way of dealing with stress was to get mad at me. He yelled and screamed at everything I did. He never asked for something; he ordered it. I chose to leave the house on weekends to escape seeing Dad. While away from home I began to enjoy art and music. The floodgates of sensuality opened up to me in my music. It eased my pain and carried me along. My escape into music, art, drugs, and myself was the beginning of the end of any chance to resolve the conflicts at home.

During tenth grade things only grew worse at school. I did find an identity as a "hippie" that I thought had some value. The trouble though was that I polarized myself even more from others who already wanted to intimidate me.

The problems in the halls of the school began. I was picked on regularly because of my long hair and clothes. My art teacher finally sensed what was going on and befriended me. So I told her what I was up against. She asked me if she could intervene, but I requested that she not do so. I knew that her involvement might only worsen my situation with my peers.

What she offered me though was a neutral zone. Whenever things got crazy and the guys tried to chase me, I would head for her class. What was great about her was not her offer of safety, but that she saw me as I was. She saw my eyes and knew when I was high. She knew where I was personally and tried to help me. Although I was taking LSD, smoking pot, and using other hallucinogenics, she pointed out the lives of certain people that we both knew who were "strung out" and destined for failure. I promised her that I would never use a needle or get into harder drugs.

Meanwhile, my parents were totally oblivious to my needs and what was going on in my life. Their family focus was so wrapped up in my ill sister that they just couldn't see my problems.

It became worse than ever between my father and me. He treated me like a dog. Every word out of his mouth was screaming and yelling. He hollered at the way I got ice out of the freezer and even the way I threw out the trash. I fought back with him and it got hot and furious.

One night I lost my cool, and screamed out just how much I hated living with him. I told him with fury and tears just how he was tearing me and the family apart. What was going on at school, with the beatings and the humiliations, also slipped out.

He had no idea. He was humbled. He tried to offer help and asked me if I wanted to move somewhere else or go in and talk to the principal. I told him there wasn't anything he could do at school for me. I told him I had to deal with these problems wherever I went.

That night passed and things seemed to improve between us at first. His abusiveness wasn't as bad, but in about a week or so it resumed. He became his old self again. . . .

This son ultimately "gave up" on trying to help his father understand him. The effects of their father-son relationship have followed him into his adulthood and hindered many of his relationships. The good news about this individual is that through a relationship with God, a loving wife and family, the establishment of some close male friends, and psychotherapy, he was able to begin believing in himself. He has now developed confidence, self-esteem, better decision-making skills, and a definite vocational direction as a result. Ironically, he has now gone back to his father and is making gradual progress in reestablishing a healthier relationship with him. It's hard work and slow going, but sometimes worth it.

The purpose of these letters and excerpts is not to assume that all relationships can or will be reconciled. However, they do show the long-term effects of both positive and negative experiences in father-son relationships. In any situation there are two sides to a story. Mistakes will be made because people are not perfect. The mistakes we make as parents often affect our children throughout their lives, but all is not lost. There are opportunities throughout life to heal old wounds and reconcile relationships that have long since been severed.

When adult children become parents, they are often surprised at how difficult it is to be a good father or mother. They begin to understand more clearly how tough it was for their own parents. Ideally, each generation develops better emotional and psychological parenting tools for rearing the next generation. However, mistakes will be made. As long as these mistakes become lessons through which we learn, it is never too late to remedy, reconcile, and redirect.

Words to Fathers:
Was your relationship with your father all that you wanted it to be? In what ways could you have been closer? What pleasant memories do you have? What regrets do you recall? How would you like things to be different between you?

If you have a desire for a closer relationship with your father or you have unfinished business with him, do not delay. If he is still alive, contact him by phone or letter. Tell him what you appreciated about your life together. Give him credit for all he did do for you. Then talk about how you would like for things to be between you in the future. From this initial contact, there will be an open door to discuss problems, regrets, or leftover attitudes.

This may not be possible if your father has progressive Alzheimer's disease, chronic alcoholism, neurological deterioration, or is deceased. In such cases, you might consider talking to a counselor or minister to decide if additional guidance would be helpful.

Regardless of whom you talk to, your father or a professional, it can strengthen your relationship with your son. The power of the past will cause us to either repeat our mistakes or learn from our lessons.

Suggestions for Sons:
Below are some specific questions sons can ask their fathers about their childhood and upbringing. They provide a very natural transition into discussing your own father-

son relationship. This can easily be done face-to-face or over the phone.

1. What was your childhood like?
2. What was your father like?
3. How did you and your father get along?
4. What significant things did you learn from him?
5. What did you both do together?
6. What do you wish could have been different between the two of you?
7. What ways do you wish he was different?
8. How has he influenced your life?
9. How do you see yourself as similar and dissimilar to him as a father?
10. What things would you do the same and differently as a father?
11. What regrets do you have as a father?
12. How are each of your sons like you?
13. How are each of your sons different than you?
14. How do you wish you were closer to your son?
15. How could I have been easier to get to know as a son?
16. How would you like our relationship to improve or change in the future?
17. What would you like to do more of together?

I talked to my dad for an hour and a half on the phone last night about fathers and sons. I asked him about his relationship with his father. He loved his dad, but they weren't as close as he wished they could have been. They had different interests and sometimes didn't know what to say to each other. Apparently they became closer after my father married my mother. He learned a lot from his dad about responsibility, loyalty, dedication, honesty, and taking care of one's family.

Parents in my grandfather's generation didn't have the benefit of the self-help books on relationships, self-esteem, and parenting that we have. They were taught to work hard, to be tough, that children should be seen and not heard, and that expressing emotions was a weakness. I remember my grandfather as a rugged policeman who liked to laugh. He used to hug my brother and I when we would visit, and his end of the day beard would always scratch our cheeks. I also remember his funeral. I never cried so much in my whole life as I did then.

I have a lot of respect for my dad. He related to me last night that as a young father he had an overwhelmingly strong desire for us to turn out right. I appreciate that about him. Sometimes he tried too hard but his heart was in the right place. Parents aren't perfect—they are doomed to imperfection from the start. I know my boys realize that about me, but I hope they see how hard I'm trying. My dad did a lot of things right. He taught us about responsibility, determination, honesty, and sports. He also made his share of mistakes. Some dads would defend their efforts with comments like, "I did the best I could." I appreciate my dad's courage. He readily acknowledged regrets he had about our upbringing. He was even eager to talk more about the past face-to-face. I can sense how important it has become to him to have a friendship with each of his sons now.

I asked my sons tonight how I could be a better dad. They both looked puzzled about why I would ask them a question like that. David, in his characteristically frank manner, spoke up first, "You could spend more time with us." Chris responded, "You do things with us when we ask, though. We think you're the best dad we could ask for." They had both had a good night at football practice so they were in fairly positive moods. Perhaps if they were mad at me about something they would not have been so kind.

After asking them a couple more times about what I could do better with little success, I gave up while I was ahead. I'm sure as they get older I will hear enough about how I have fouled up. But for now I will be grateful that things seem to be going well between us and remember to keep an ear open for the rockier times that will eventually be ahead. Maybe God's love and my willingness to do whatever it takes will help them forgive my blunders.

Thank goodness God is in control.

Organizations Providing Healing for the Homosexual

Homosexuals Anonymous
H.A. Fellowship Services
P.O. Box 7881-B
Reading, PA 19603
1-800-253-3000

Eleutheros
1298 Minnesota
Suite D
Winter Park, FL 32789
404-629-5770

Exodus International-North America
P.O. Box 2121
San Rafael, CA 94912
415-454-1017

Love In Action
P.O. Box 2655
San Rafael, CA 94912
415-454-0960

For an audio cassette on "Treatment of Dystonic Homosexuality," send a check for $12.00 to Dr. D. Charles Williams, 1864 Independent Square, Suite AB, Dunwoody, GA 30338.

Chapter 1

1. M. Segell, "The American Man in Transition," *American Health* (January 1990): 59–61.
2. Ibid.

Chapter 2

1. Beth Spring, "Having It All—At Home," *Focus on the Family,* 19 Oct. 1989, 5–7.
2. Tim Hansel, *What Kids Need Most in a Dad* (Old Tappan, N.J.: Fleming H. Revell, 1989), 19–31.

Chapter 4

1. Scott Walker, *The Freedom Factor: Overcoming Barriers to Being Yourself* (San Francisco: Harper and Row, Publishers, 1989).
2. Tim Hansel, *What Kids Need Most in a Dad* (Old Tappan, N.J.: Fleming H. Revell, 1989), 129–30.
3. Ibid., 142.
4. Ibid., 172–75.

Chapter 5

1. James Buie, "Men Struggle to Define New Role, Drop Clichés," *American Psychological Association Monitor* (Aug. 1989): 29.

2. K. Druck and J. Simmons, *Secrets Men Keep.* Doubleday. 1985. 35–36.
3. Ibid., 39–40.

Chapter 6

1. M. Busico, "Self-Centeredness of Adults Blamed for Children's Plight," *The Atlanta Journal and Constitution,* 10 Nov. 1989, sec. B.
2. D. Brewster, "The Lesson of Kilimanjaro," *Focus on the Family,* June 1989, 6–9.

Chapter 7

1. "Hypermasculinity Challenged by Gottman, Napier, Pittman," *Family Therapy News* (Dec. 1989): 16.

Chapter 9

1. S. Keen and O. Zur, "Who Is the New Ideal Man?" *Psychology Today,* Nov. 1989, 54–60.
2. H. Freudenberger, "Today's Troubled Men," *Psychology Today,* Dec. 1987, 46–47.
3. Bobbie Reed, *Single Mothers Raising Sons* (Nashville: Thomas Nelson, Inc. Publishers, 1988), 138–43.

Chapter 10

1. "The Future of Gay America," *Newsweek,* 12 March 1990, 20–25.
2. James Buie, "Men Only Therapy Programs Emerge," *The American Psychological Association Monitor* (March 1990): 16–17.

3. Eric McCollum, "Between Fathers and Sons," *Menninger Perspective*, no. 2 (1989).
4. Tim LaHaye, *What Everyone Should Know About Homosexuality* (Wheaton, Ill.: Tyndale House Publishers, 1985), 74.
5. James Buie, "Heterosexual Ethic Mentality Is Decried," *The American Psychological Association Monitor* (March 1990): 20.
6. D. Bjorklund and B. Bjorklund, "Straight or Gay?" *Parents*, October 1988, 93–98.
7. Ibid.
8. Elizabeth Moberly, *Homosexuality: A New Christian Ethic* Cambridge, England: James Clark and Co. LTD., 1986.
9. Reed, *Single Mothers*.
10. J. Money, "Sin, Sickness, or Status? Homosexual Gender Identity and Psychoneuroendocrinology," *American Psychologist* (April 1987): 384–99.
11. T. Adler, "Differences Explored in Gays and Straights," *The American Psychological Asssociation Monitor* (January 1990): 27.
12. Buie, "Heterosexual Ethic."